The Word Whiz's
Guide to
Massachusetts Elementary School Vocabulary

By Chris Kensler

A Paper Airplane Project

Simon & Schuster
New York ● London ● Sydney ● Singapore ● Toronto

Kaplan Publishing
Published by Simon & Schuster, Inc.
1230 Avenue of the Americas
New York, NY 10020

For bulk sales to schools, colleges, and universities, please contact: Order Department,
Simon & Schuster, 100 Front Street, Riverside, NJ 08075. Phone: 1-800-223-2336. Fax:
1-800-943-9831.

Cover Design: Cheung Tai
Interior Page Design and Production: Heather Kern

Manufactured in the United States of America

January 2002

10 9 8 7 6 5 4 3 2 1

Library of Congress Cataloging-in-Publication Data

ISBN 0-7432-1102-2

All of the practice questions in this book were created by the authors to illustrate
question types. They are not actual test questions.

Table of Contents

About the Author

Chris Kensler grew up in Indiana and attended Indiana University, where he majored in English. He has worked as an educational book editor, covered the presidential campaign for a major news organization, run a national digital arts and culture magazine, and written several titles for kids, including *Study Smart Junior*, which received the Parents' Choice Award.

Red Schox is a figment of his imagination.

Acknowledgments

The author would like to thank Maureen McMahon and Lori DeGeorge for their help in shaping and editing the manuscript.

The publisher wishes to thank Margaret Rodero and Ryan Blanchette for their contributions to this book.

Dedication

For Louise Sebene

Introduction

Hi. My name is Red. Red Schox. Please, keep your jokes to yourself. I have heard them all.

I am in the fifth grade. I live in, you guessed it, Boston, Massachusetts. I am a baseball fanatic, a pretty good soccer player, and a vocabulary whiz kid. You name the word, I know its definition. Especially the words they use on the MCAS (Massachusetts Comprehensive Assessment System) tests. As a matter of fact, any word you are supposed to know by the fifth grade—I know it. But I'm not here to brag. I'm here to help.

I am here for parents, guardians, siblings, and teachers of elementary-school kids in the great state of Massachusetts—for everyone who wants to help students learn the vocabulary words they need to know. Let me be your guide to Word Whiz-ardry.

And if I can't turn your student into a vocabulary whiz like me, I can at least teach her some really important words—words that will help her in school, on the MCAS tests, and in life.

Why Students Blank on Tests

Some kids mess up on tests because they don't understand the question, not because they don't know the answer. My good friend Larry reads all the time, but when he comes across a test question like "What is the best summary of this story?" he gets nervous, because all the answers look pretty good. My other friend Judith is a math whiz, but just last week she got stumped on a math problem that asked her which number was "greatest." She thought it meant which number was really, really cool, not which number was the "biggest."

This is where *Word Whiz* comes in. This book builds a bridge from the words your student does know to the ones used on all kinds of tests. Learning vocabulary this way makes it easier to remember and harder to forget.

Building a bridge is an active thing, so these are active exercises. They do not involve straight memorization–that's been proven to be a bad way for your student to remember words for anything longer than a day. *Word Whiz* exercises involve doing fun things like watching TV, reading magazines, drawing, and using one's imagination.

Lots of the exercises are also designed to become a part of your student's everyday life—as much a part as soccer or band practice. That way, the

WhizTip
Hey you—the adult who bought this book—way to go! Education is a team game. Just like Nomar Garciaparra needs the rest of the Red Sox to help him win the pennant, your kid needs a team to help him learn.

WhizTip

When you write exercise questions for your student, always give her four possible answer choices, just like on the MCAS.

words can seep deep into the brain, so not only are you preparing your student for the MCAS tests, but for all the big tests to come.

How to Use This Book

The book is divided into two parts—the Word Whiz exercises and Word Whiz vocabulary lists. The exercises cover words in five major categories: Test Instructions, English Language Arts, Mathematics, History and Social Science, and Science and Technology/Engineering. Off to the side of the exercises, you'll see a series of icons. These tell you what "materials" the exercises employ—TV, magazines, the Internet, etc. Here they are:

| Life | School | Movie | Sports | Magazine |
| History | Imagination | News | Internet | Television |

On each exercise page, I also provide a **WhizTip,** a **WhizWord,** or an **On the MCAS** tip. A **WhizTip** gives more information on how you can help your student. A **WhizWord** is an extra vocabulary word related to the ones covered in the exercise. An **On the MCAS** tip shows you how the vocabulary word has been used on the state assessment.

Lots of the exercises involve writing a story or a sample sentence. Not only will this help with learning the words, it will also help your student improve his writing skills. For this book, and for all schoolwork, your student should:

- Write legibly
- Use complete sentences with appropriate punctuation and capitalization
- Spell the words correctly
- Use the correct verb tenses
- Use singular and plural forms of regular nouns and adjust verbs for agreement

The Word Whiz vocabulary lists at the back of the book have everyday definitions for the most important words. If your student hasn't heard of some of these words yet, don't panic! It's possible he hasn't made it to that stage in his curriculum yet. If you are working with a second or third grader, just make sure you discuss the words he doesn't know. This will give him an advantage when they start using these words on a regular basis in class.

But enough of my yakkin'—let's boogie.

All-Purpose
WhizCards: Part I

In this age of computers, the Internet, and the Sony PlayStation, it's hard to believe that one of the best ways to review words is still the old 3 x 5 flashcard. I keep waiting for Nintendo to come out with something on the Gameboy to replace flashcards, but it hasn't happened yet.

Flashcards work for a few reasons. Reason 1: By writing down the word and its definition on the card, your student's brain has a better chance of storing it than it does simply by reading the word. Reason 2: Flashcards are a good way to whittle down a large group of words to the ones your student is really having trouble with. If she starts out with 100 flashcards and after a couple run-throughs is only having trouble with 30 of them, you both know which words to focus on. Reason 3: They are portable. Your student can take them anywhere anytime. A few minutes of review on the way to the store, dinner out, or a baseball card signing quickly start to add up.

WhizTip

It is extremely important for you to praise your student for his progress and, if possible, set up an awards system for this exercise. (My dad gives me baseball cards.) Make it something he looks forward to, not a chore.

MAKING WHIZCARDS

Get a pack of colorful index cards. Choose one color and one of the five categories of vocabulary words in this book (Test Instructions, English Language Arts, Math, History and Social Science, and Science and Technology/Engineering). It can be a subject you are both interested in or a subject in which your student needs to build her confidence.

Have your student print each WhizWord in large, legible letters on one side of an index card. Talk about the word. Have your student use it in a sentence. Try to think of clues or tricks she can use to remember it. Now you (the adult) write the definition and any clues or sentences your student came up with on the reverse side. (Use your best handwriting like they taught you in school all those years ago.)

Try to make 20-25 WhizCards a day, completing one subject before moving on to the next, until you have a complete set of WhizCards. (You can do more if your student is enjoying herself, fewer if she is getting stressed.)

By making these WhizCards, you will automatically improve your student's familiarity and comfort with a lot of new words. You will also know which words (and subjects) she needs the most work on. And, most importantly, you will be able to play the cool games on the next page.

All-Purpose
WhizCards: Part II

WhizTip

Remember, your student has enough worries in his life—probably more than you did at his age. Try to keep your vocabulary work with him as enjoyable as humanly possible.

Ever since my parents got the deluxe cable package, I've been watching the Game Show Network. It has reruns of classic game shows from the '60s, '70s and '80s. The clothes worn by the game show hosts and contestants are . . . incredible. Where did people get the idea that big pointy collars and lots of chest hair are attractive? Anyway, all of the classic game shows have given me a couple of classic ideas for games you and your student can play using WhizCards.

PLAYING WHIZCARD GAMES

Guess Again!
You need 2-4 players (two on each team) and a stopwatch or egg timer to play. One person on each team picks five WhizCards. That player tries to get the other person on the team to guess what the word on the WhizCard is by giving clues, without saying the word. The clue-giver can—and should!—say the definition, and think up other hints.

Each team has one minute to try to get through all five WhizCards. For example, after the first round, the score could be "three words correct" to "two words correct" (3-2). Each team then picks five more words and the team members switch places (the one who was guessing is now giving the clues). You keep playing like this until one team gets 20 words correct.

But you can also play Guess Again! with just two people. If you do, see how long (how many minutes) it takes to get 20 words correct. Play the game regularly and try to beat your own best record. (Note: It's important to discuss the words your team couldn't figure out after each round.)

Whiz Draw
To play, you need 2-10 players, a stopwatch or egg timer, and a big pad of paper. (Whiz Draw is best played with one of those big poster-sized pads of paper, but a regular-size notebook works, too.) Divide the players into two teams. One player on each team picks out five WhizCards. That "artist" has two minutes to draw pictures that provide clues for each word. The artist cannot speak or write any words! Keep playing, alternating between the teams, until one team gets 20 words correct.

Whiz Draw is the most fun when you play with lots of friends and family members, but you can play it with just two people. If you do, see how long it takes you to get 20 words correct, with you and your student switching every five words from "artist" to "word-guesser." Play the game regularly and try to beat your own best record, and discuss the words your student couldn't figure out.

Test Instructions
Close Enough

Usually, when I'm taking a test, I'm trying to find the exact right answer. But sometimes, tests only ask students to find an answer that is **probably** right. For example, there may be a reading passage about a boy named Roy who thinks that beets are really neat. The question could say:

Which word describes how Roy **probably** feels about beets?

> A. sad
> B. mad
> C. glad
> D. afraid

Now, the story may not have said anything about Roy actually getting happy or glad when he sees a beet, but he thinks they are neat, so "glad" is **most likely** how he feels. It's close enough—much closer than "sad" and "mad" for sure, while "afraid" makes absolutely no sense at all.

The key to spotting these "Close Enough" words is reading the question carefully. If your student rushes through it, he could become frightened when the exact right answer just isn't there! And, speaking of beets, a good place for your student to get used to spotting things that are close enough is at dinner.

WhizTip

Your attitude is important. Pay attention to what your student is saying. Show her that you choose words carefully to convey a specific meaning. Show her that you pay close attention to her word choices.

PLAYING WITH FOOD

You will need a notebook or a piece of paper and a pencil for this exercise. (I suggest a notebook, so you can keep it handy for some of the other exercises in this book.) Now, have your student look at his food. Ask him a few questions about his meal, using the words on the list above. Ask him to think about what other food is *similar* to what he is eating. If you are having pot roast, have him think about what food is the *best* substitute for it. (A steak is *similar* to pot roast because it is also a piece of beef.) If you are eating spaghetti, you can ask your student what foods you would *probably* fix to go with spaghetti. (Garlic bread and a tossed salad come to mind.) If you have prepared a wonderful tray of spicy enchiladas, you can ask your student what he will *most likely* need after a few bites. (Water!)

Have your student write down his answers to your questions in complete sentences in the notebook, using the words and phrases at the top of this page. So, for example, he would write "I will *most likely* need a glass of Mountain Dew to put out the fire in my mouth caused by Dad's enchiladas." Do this at every family meal, rotating the "Close Enough" words every night until he has written sentences including each of them three times (three meals). For added incentive, consider this: No write-a the sentence, no eat-a the food! (At least that's how my Italian grandmother would put it.)

Test Instructions

Answer Clues

On the MCAS
Who are the main characters in this story?
A. Bill and Ted
B. Punch and Judy
C. Marge and Homer
D. Cats and dogs

Up until last year, my favorite reporter was Clark Kent of the Daily Planet. Then I started watching the news on cable with my dad. Now my favorite reporter is CNN's Wolf Blitzer. He even has this cool beard/moustache combo that makes him look like a wolf. (I wonder what came first, the look or the name?) Anyway, the reason I like him is he makes even boring stuff sound exciting. Say there's a Senate hearing about a spending bill on Capitol Hill. That's boring. But when Wolf tells the story, it's like there's a tornado tearing down your street and if you don't get in the basement *now*, you are toast!

Another reason I like Wolf is he sticks to the five W's that every good reporter knows by heart: **who**, **what**, **where**, **when**, and **why**. Those five W's also just happen to be the five answer clues a student should be looking for in test questions. (Isn't it cool how that worked out?)

CUB REPORTER

Part 1
Find a newspaper or magazine article about something your student is interested in. After reading it, write three multiple choice questions using the "Answer Clues" words. For instance, if the article was about a concert by the rock group the Red Hot Chili Peppers, you could ask:

Where did the Chili Peppers play their concert?
A. The 4-H Fairgrounds
B. The Fleet Center
C. To benefit the Red Cross
D. Flea

Where is the answer clue in this question. It tells you the answer is a place, which automatically rules out answers C and D. (C is a reason, which could only be an answer to a *why* question. D is a person: the band's bass player—an answer to a *who* question.) By reading the article he should be able to choose between the two *where* answers, A and B.

Part 2
Have your student choose a family event and write a short news report on it. It could be "Our Cat Lou Went to the Vet" or "My Mom Had Her Friend Jerry Over for Coffee." Have your student write a five paragraph report, with each of the paragraphs labeled *who*, *what*, *where*, *when*, and *why*. This will help your student get even better at spotting the five W's in test questions.

Alternate parts 1 and 2 every week until your student has the five W's mastered.

Test Instructions

Ups and Downs

Despite all the joy I give my parents, they give me only $10 a week for my allowance. Dad calls it my "base pay." That means I can still get more money for doing big jobs around the house, like mowing the lawn ($10), weeding the garden ($5), and packing up the recyclables ($2). So my allowance actually goes up and down each week, depending on how many extra chores I do. For instance, this week I have raked in $25 by mowing the lawn and painting part of the fence.

Unfortunately, my spending also fluctuates wildly. I am already down from $25 to $3.50, thanks to four hours of serious game-playing at Two-Bit Bandit (the local arcade). Looks like I better get to that weeding.

WhizTip

Remember! When you ask your student these test-type questions, write them down whenever you can. Your student needs to see the words on paper, not just hear them, so she recognizes them on the test.

TRACKING HIGHS AND LOWS

For this exercise, your student is going to track the highs and lows of a particular number. I'll use spending money as the example, but she can track any number: the batting or scoring average of a favorite player; the stock market; television ratings; or the online sales ranking of her favorite book.

Using spending money as an example: Every night before she goes to bed, have your student count her money and write down how much she has. At the end of one week, have her give you the money chart and write out questions for her that use all seven "Ups and Downs" words. Here are a couple of examples:

On which day did your funds *decrease* the most?
A. Monday
B. Tuesday
C. Wednesday
D. Thursday

What day was your fund's *highest* point?
A. Wednesday
B. Thursday
C. Friday
D. Saturday

If your student has trouble with the questions, repeat the exercise the following week using a different set of numbers (stock market, book sales ranking). Keep it up until she gets all your questions right.

Test Instructions
Facts and Opinions

On the MCAS

Using the clues provided, pick the correct figure:

A. triangle
B. rectangle
C. trapezoid
D. hexagon

When your student is reading about stuff she likes, it's pretty easy for her to remember what she just read. For example, I'm a Red Sox fan. I just read the biography of Red Sox legend Ted Williams. It told how "The Kid" hit .406 in 1941, was voted onto eighteen All-Star teams, and how he absolutely hates neckties (me too!). If you ask me a question about that book and give me four answer choices, I'm probably going to pick the right one.

But let's say you ask me questions about something or someone I find really boring—like Christina Aguilera. It is harder to figure out the **facts** and **opinions** in a story you have no interest in. How am I supposed to remember what her favorite song is on her new album? I could care less! However, in order to succeed on the MCAS and other tests, your student needs to be able to distinguish between **facts** and **opinions**, whether she is interested in the reading passage or not.

READING THE REVIEWS

You are going to use reading materials that your student actually likes to get your student used to separating *facts* from *opinions*, and to make familiar the words *correct* and *true*.

Pick out a piece of writing that has both *facts* and *opinions*. I suggest movie, music, book, and television reviews.

Your student is going to:
1) Answer two questions about the review.
2) Pick out one *fact* from the review.
3) Pick out one *opinion* from the review.

So first, you need to write down a *fact/opinion* question and a *correct/true* question. Here is an example, using a review of my favorite cartoon, *Digimon*:

Which of the following is the *opinion* of the writer?
A. *Digimon* is a good show.
B. *Digimon* is a bad show.
C. *Digimon* is going off the air.
D. *Digimon* is on too early.

According to the review, which statement is *true*?
A. *Digimon* is really popular.
B. *Digimon* is not popular at all.
C. *Digimon* is a show about snails.
D. *Digimon* is going to be made into a movie.

Have your student read the review and tackle your questions. Then ask your student to identify one additional *fact* and *opinion* in the review. Do this with three reviews, or until you are confident your student is comfortable with the "Facts and Opinions" words.

Test Instructions

Explanations

Sometimes, I get in trouble. In fact, just yesterday my mom got upset with me. All I did was turn my sister Rose's favorite Red Sox hat into a cozy bed for my hamster Nomar. My mom said, "What **clue** could I have had that you were going to do such a thing?" I could have mentioned that I asked her where Rose's hat was, and that I asked her if she thought Nomar needed a new bed, that I asked her if she thought a baseball hat would make a good hamster bed. If mom had been taking a test, she would have failed, because she totally missed all of the **evidence** of my plan.

Indeed, tests are always asking students to find **evidence** to support a theory; to provide **reasons** for their answers; to search for **clues** to solve a puzzle; and to base their answers on a set of **examples**.

On the MCAS

This story is an
example of a:

A. poem
B. essay
C. fable
D. tall tale

EXPLAIN IT AWAY

For this exercise, you are going to write for your student a question about his recent behavior and have him support his answer with *examples, reasons,* and *evidence.*

For example, regarding the hamster/hat incident, my mother could ask me:

Do you think it is okay to use your sister's property to make Nomar more comfortable? Please provide *evidence* to support your answer.

And I would answer:

Yes. It is okay to use my sister's property to make Nomar more comfortable. I once used her T-shirt as a rag to clean his aquarium, and she often gives me the carrots from her lunch box to feed Nomar.

Of course there is no reason to focus on the negative. You can also ask questions about good behavior, like:

Please give three *reasons* your grades have improved so much over the last month.

If he has trouble answering any of your questions, provide him a *clue* to the answer. For this question you could write:

Clue: How much TV were you watching a month ago? How much are you watching now?

Do this exercise once a week until you have used each of the "Explain Yourself" words three times.

Test Instructions
Order of Events

On the MCAS

According to this encyclopedia entry, which happened first:

A. Invention of paper
B. Invention of pencils
C. Invention of printing press
D. Invention of salad

Some test questions work to make sure students can relate one event to another. Which events come **before** and **after** another event? What number belongs **between** 5 and 9 in this number pattern? The words are pretty easy to use in everyday conversation. ("I'm **after** you on the PlayStation!"; "Have you heard the **first** single off the new 'N Sync CD?") But when your student sees these words on a test, they can get really confusing.

Using Massachusetts history can help you accomplish two goals at the same time. By learning her "Order of Events" words while reviewing Massachusetts history, your student gets to know the words, and she also gets to know a little more about her state, which could also help on a history test sometime.

STATE HISTORY TIMELINES

In grade school, kids learn a lot about where they live. For instance, they know that colonists staged the Boston Tea party in 1773 to protest the tax England put on their beloved beverage. But how many know that, in 1919, 21 people died when 2.2 million gallons of molasses flooded part of downtown Boston? And how many know that in 1974, scientists at the Army's Natick Labs accidentally released turtle-sized Giant Hissing Madagascar cockroaches into a Randolph, Massachusetts dump? The roaches quickly made their way into Boston-area homes and had to be killed with DDT!

These kinds of bizarre events can help your student learn the words used to describe the order of events. (A good source for bizarre Boston information is Bizarro Boston at www.boston-online.com/bizarro.html.) Use some little known facts like these, along with a "standard" history source, to make a timeline covering ten historical events. (A timeline is a long, horizontal line with evenly spaced dots that indicate years or dates on the timeline.) When you are done, write six questions that pertain to the timeline, with each question using one of the "Order of Events" words.

For example, if you were using some of the events mentioned above, you could ask:

What happened *after* Kennedy was inaugurated president in 1960?
A. 21 people died in a molasses flood in 1918.
B. Scientists released giant cockroaches in 1974.
C. Bill Russell won his first championship with the Celtics in 1957.
D. Colonists staged the Boston Tea Party in 1773.

Answer: B.

If your student has trouble with any of the words, repeat the exercise with another timeline, writing questions that use only the "Order of Events" words she had trouble with.

Test Instructions

Quantities

Students expect to see numbers and measurements on math and science tests, but history tests use them too on questions about important dates, the length of time wars lasted, and the distances explorers traveled to find new lands. So students are constantly solving problems involving all kinds of quantities—length, weight, volume, time, etc. That makes it extremely important for kids to know measurement terms and their abbreviations.

Here is a list of measurements that commonly appear on all kinds of tests, along with their common abbreviations. An exercise follows which will help your student get on good terms with these terms.

COMMON MEASUREMENTS AND THEIR ABBREVIATIONS

LENGTH (abbr.)		VOLUME (abbr.)		WEIGHT (abbr.)		TIME (abbr.)	
(Imperial)		(Imperial)		(Imperial)			
inch	in	ounce	oz	ounce	oz	second	sec
foot	ft	quart	qt	pound	lb	minute	min
mile	mi	gallon	gal			hour	hr
						year	yr
(Metric)		(Metric)		(Metric)		morning	AM
centimeter	cm	milliliter	ml	gram	g	evening	PM
meter	m	liter	l	kilogram	kg		
kilometer	km						

QUALITY QUANTITY TIME

You've heard of spending quality time with your student. This exercise takes that idea one step further. Declare fifteen minutes of your day Quality Quantity Time. Pick a time in each day when both you and your student are normally together talking about stuff, like in the car after school, on the way to music lessons or soccer practice, or during dinner. During Quality Quantity Time, for everything that you say or do that has a quantity attached to it, ask your student to identify the quantity term and its abbreviation.

For example, if you are driving to the mall, you can ask "What's the best measurement for the distance from here to the mall?" If your student says "miles" or "kilometers," he got it right. Tell him how many miles or kilometers it is to the mall, then ask him what the abbreviation is. If, on the other hand, your student says "feet" or "inches," explain that those are indeed distance measures, but they are used for shorter things like tables and books. If he answers "ounces," well, you've got even more explaining to do! (See the WhizTip for some other examples.)

Keep this up until your student has all of the common measurements and their abbreviations ready at the tip of his tongue.

Whiz Tip
Some everyday activities you can use for this exercise:

car trips
(distance)

appointments
(time)

getting groceries
(volume)

cleaning house
(weight)

eating
(volume/weight)

exercising
(distance)

watching TV
(time)

English Language Arts
Parts of Speech

Come close. A little closer. Wait, you're crowding me, back up a bit. Perfect. I have something important to tell you. Not only should your student learn what all these vocabulary words mean, he should also learn what parts of speech the words are.

No big deal—there are only a few parts of speech. It's not like we're dealing with Egyptian hieroglyphs—where every picture represents a totally different thing.

LABELING PARTS OF SPEECH

Have your student photocopy a page out of her favorite book or magazine. It can be *Harry Potter, Ranger Rick*—whatever. Now pick three sentences and have your student copy them onto lined paper, with a blank line separating each line of the sentence. Have her label every word on that page with a part of speech.

To make sure your student sticks with it, do this exercise with her, armed with this book (all the parts of speech in the list above are explained in the back of the book) and your trusty *Elements of Style* (if you need it). When she comes to a word she doesn't know, discuss it and figure out what kind of word it must be. Here's an example from a story on the NASCAR website:

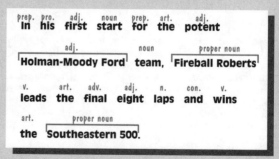

prep.	pro.	adj.	noun	prep.	art.	adj.
In	his	first	start	for	the	potent

adj.	noun	proper noun
Holman-Moody Ford	team,	Fireball Roberts

v.	art.	adv.	adj.	n.	con.	v.
leads	the	final	eight	laps	and	wins

art.	proper noun
the	Southeastern 500.

Repeat this exercise with three different pieces of reading material. Different kinds of writing use different kinds of words. Newspapers use a bunch of *verbs* and *proper nouns*. Fiction uses a bunch of *adjectives* and *adverbs*. Show your student how to check her answers using the parts-of-speech labels in a dictionary.

<u>Important:</u> Don't do all three sample passages in a row. Do them over the course of a few days or a week. That way she will have time to learn the parts of speech at a pace that lets her brain absorb them. Spreading things out will also keep her from running away screaming!

Words Covered

character, detail, dialogue, hero, heroine, imagery, metaphor, moral, narrator, personification, plot, point of view, scene, setting, simile, theme

English Language Arts
Writing Tools

I like to write my own stories. I won a young writers fiction award last year for a story I wrote about a cricket and his adventures in Beantown. I titled it "Chirpie and Paul." Chirpie the Cricket is the **narrator**. He has to find his city cousin, Paul, because their grandfather passed on (bass bait!) and left them in his will the map to the best vegetable gardens in Salem. That's the **plot**. Paul becomes the story's **hero** when he rescues Chirpie from the clutches of Carl the Evil Bluejay. They both live happily ever after, munching on the leaves of Farmer Ted's tomato plants.

Anyway, to write my story I used a bunch of the writing tools all writers use. Its important for your student to know what those tools are. Things like **narrator, plot, hero, dialogue, imagery**—they're all parts of what make stories fun to read.

WhizTip

If your student is unfamiliar with more than three to four of these words, do the story-writing exercise several times, using three to four words each time.

SHORT STORY WRITING

Go over the "Writing Tools" words with your student to gauge his familiarity with them. Mark the ones he has trouble with. Use the word list in the back of this book to introduce your student to any words that are new to him. Write those words and their definitions down on a piece of paper.

Now set your student up with a pencil and paper or a new Word document on his computer. Give him thirty minutes to write a piece of fiction about his favorite subject. It can be about a superhero who does laundry, a pet cat who does good deeds for strangers, a cricket who visits Boston—anything. Supply your student with the list of words he had trouble with. Have him write his story, focusing on using the writing tools he didn't know.

The words should not be part of the story, but he should use them to tell his story. For example, if he had trouble with *imagery* and *metaphor*, he needs to use a LOT of *imagery* and a TON of *metaphors* in his story. The story doesn't need to win any awards, it just needs to show he knows what the words mean.

<u>Note</u>: You can also point out examples of these concepts when you are watching TV, in magazines that your student reads, and in movies. (If you point them out during a movie, keep your voice down.)

English Language Arts

Answer Words

Leave it to tests to make reading scary. Not only do we kids have to read things we wouldn't otherwise touch with a ten-foot pole, but we also have to explain what we just read! And they aren't easy questions either. The MCAS tests tell us to "**support** your theory" or "**summarize** the third paragraph" or "**paraphrase** the writer's opinion of green eggs and ham." It's enough to make a young reader long for the days of *See Spot Run*.

But those simple times are gone forever. So it is important for you to make sure your student knows what these "Answer Words" mean. All of these "Answer Words" ask the reader to become actively involved with what she just read, which is kind of what this book does. The best way to get her used to doing this on tests is to get her used to doing it with reading material she actually likes.

FINDING THE ANSWERS

Ask your student to pick out two different pieces of reading material. It can be the latest *TV Guide*, a back issue of *Car & Driver*, Leo Tolstoy's *War and Peace*—whatever. Now you choose one short reading passage from each. Keep it short—no longer than one page.

Read each passage yourself and write down three questions. For example, for a *Soap Opera Digest* story about a hot young actor, you could write:

1. *Summarize* why Ben Starrington thinks he will be the next Tom Cruise."
2. *Paraphrase* Ben Starrington's acting technique.
3. *Support* the theory that Ben Starrington is an idiot.

Have your student write a response to each question. Check them. In all cases, it is important for your student to base her response on details from the reading passage. Her answers should identify the sections in the reading passage that support her conclusions. For example:

<u>*Support* the theory that Ben Starrington is an idiot.</u>
Ben Starrington is obviously a doofus because he thinks Leo Tolstoy is the actor who played the Cowardly Lion in the *Wizard of Oz*, he thinks Christina Aguilera has a better voice than Barbra Streisand, and his favorite food is wheat germ.

Words Covered

author, autobiography, biography, essay, fable, fantasy, fiction, folklore, genre, limerick, nonfiction, poem, tall tale

English Language Arts
Literary Genres

There are many different kinds of writing, but they can be roughly grouped into three categories: true stories, make-believe stories, and **poems**.

By true stories—also called **nonfiction**—I mean stories based on facts. For example, **biographies** and **autobiographies** are based on real lives. (I just finished reading a **biography** of legendary Celtics forward John Havlicek. It was great.) **Essays** are also examples of **nonfiction**: an **essay** is a short piece of writing on a subject like "My Favorite Basketball Player" or "What I Did Last Summer."

Make-believe stories—also called **fiction**—include **fantasy** and **fables**. (The *Harry Potter* series is a perfect example of **fantasy fiction**.) And then there is **poetry**. One thing to remember about **poems** is that they usually rhyme, but not always. (I know, not much of a rule, but it's the best I can do.)

When your student is tackling a reading comprehension passage on a test, he needs to note what kind of writing it is. That will help him answer questions about it.

WhizTip

The more time you spend in libraries and bookstores with your student, the more comfortable he will feel with books, reading, and using new words.

THE HUNT FOR GENRES

For this exercise, you are going to need books. Lots of them. So get in a plane, train, or automobile and get yourself and your student over to the library or your local bookstore.

You are going to be sending your student on a series of treasure hunts while you sit back and sip a cafe latte or thumb through a newspaper. Send him out into the library or bookstore or your house to find one example of each of the "Literary Genres" words. For example, send him out to find a book of *poems* and a book of *tall tales*. Depending on how well your student knows these words, you can explain what each one means before your student goes on his search. When he brings the books back, ask him why he chose each one.

Keep sending him out on these scavenger hunts until he has located each of the literary genres. (Note: He can also ask bookstore salespeople or a librarian for help along the way—just make sure your student is the one doing the talking, not you.) As a reward, check out or purchase the book he likes best. My mom did this with me—that's how I got the Havlicek *biography*!

Words Covered
complete sentence,
compound sentence,
incomplete sentence,
interrogative sentence,
run-on sentence

English Language Arts

Sentences

Being able to write well is important in school and in lots of jobs, too. For example, my mom is a technical writer. She writes instructions and training manuals for a big electronics company. She has made it her personal mission in life to write the perfect DVD instruction manual—one that actually makes sense to a normal person.

So in her quest to show you how to use your DVD player, she tries hard to avoid using any **run-on sentences** or any **incomplete sentences. Run-on sentences** get really, really confusing because they are so long and often contain too much information. **Incomplete sentences** are jarring because they are missing a part of speech (usually a verb).

It is just as important for your student to avoid using **incomplete** and **run-on sentences** as well. It is also important for her to be able to identify them on a test.

WRITE THE INSTRUCTIONS

Grab a pencil and paper. For this exercise, you are going to give your student a mission: to write an instruction book on how to use a piece of electronic equipment. If you have a DVD, VCR, or CD player, go with that. If you have a stereo, TV, or radio, those all work, too. Even a microwave or an electric toothbrush will do!

Once you have picked a piece of electronics, choose a function. Start with an easy one, like "How to Turn on Your DVD Player." Have your student write a numbered instruction list using *complete sentences* and *interrogative sentences*. Like this:

> 1. Check to make sure the DVD player is plugged in.
> 2. Is it hooked up to the TV? Check to make sure that it is.
> 3. Once you know it is plugged in and hooked up, press the Power button.

Once your student is done, check her work for *run-on* and *incomplete sentences*. When you see one, mark it, discuss why it is either *incomplete* or a *run-on*, and ask her to rewrite the sentence as a *complete* or *compound sentence*. (If you or your student are uncertain of any of these sentence types, check their definitions in the English Language Arts word list in the back of the book.) Repeat this exercise by writing directions for the machine's other functions, like:

- How to play a DVD/CD/tape
- How to record a show/song
- How to set the clock/timer

If your student comes up with particularly easy-to-understand directions, send them to the company that makes the product. Maybe the company will replace their confusing instructions with her clear ones!

Math

Number Relationships

There are four math words that mean similar things and are easy to get confused: **mean, median, mode,** and **average**. Let's just quickly review.

- **Mean** and **average** are the same thing—it is what you get by adding some numbers together, then dividing by how many numbers you added up.
- **Median** is the middle one in a group of numbers. The same amount of numbers are above it and below it.
- The **mode** is the one that occurs the most number of times.

To help your student remember these, we are going to use a couple techniques. First, let's use some word association.

- **Mean** "means" **average**, and **average** "means" **mean**. That's the way to help your student remember those two are the same thing.
- **Median** is the middle number. Think of a **median** that divides a highway or boulevard. It runs right down the middle of the road. So does the **median** in a set of numbers—it is the number in the middle.
- **Mode** sounds like the word "most." The **mode** is the number that occurs most often in a set.

WhizTip

If there is an even number of values being considered, the median of those numbers is the average of the two numbers in the middle.

RECENT TEST SCORE RELATIONSHIPS

Now that your student has an easy way to remember which one is which, he can practice recognizing them. All you need now are sets of numbers. Test scores will do nicely!

Have him gather up all of his tests for a particular class. It can be for any class, but why not use math class as long as you're at it. Sort them from lowest to highest scores and find the values above. For example, I just gathered my math tests and quizzes for the last marking period. Here are my scores from lowest to highest:

34, 71, 83, 83, 92, 99, 99, 99, 110 (I got extra credit on that one)

Mean and *Average*	= (34+71+83+83+92+99+99+99+110) ÷ 9
	= 85.56
Median	= 92 (this test score is the middle value)
Mode	= 99 (this test score occurs 3 times)

Do this for the tests from three different classes. If your student's school doesn't give percentages, or you would rather not use test scores, you can also use a baseball team's batting averages; the points or rebounds for the players on a basketball team; or a quarterback's passing attempts and completions for a series of games.

Math
Kinds of Numbers

On the MCAS

Using the chart above, is it more likely Bob put his finger on an even number or an odd number? A negative number or a positive number?

My mom and dad have always been obsessed with gasoline prices. And with the recent turmoil surrounding high energy costs, their obsession has gotten even worse. My dad will drive for miles and miles to save two cents a gallon. I try to point out that perhaps driving all those extra miles and using all of that extra gas might counteract how much he is saving, but it doesn't seem to make an impression.

My mom has gotten into the habit of going to a website that has the current gas prices at local gas stations before she goes out to fuel up. This plan seems more rational to me. Unfortunately, she drives a big SUV that guzzles gas, so she is on that website a lot. Unless gas prices drop really fast, or my parents sell their big cars for subcompacts, trying to minimize the cost of gas is going to be a big family project for the foreseeable future.

GAS PRICE NUMBERS
The almost-daily ritual of pumping gas is a great time to work on "Kinds of Numbers" vocabulary. First, review the definitions of these words with your student. Then, whenever you pull into a gas station with your student in tow, ask her these kinds of questions.

Identifying Digits and Numerals
Ask your student to identify *digits* in the gas price. For example:

Premium gas costs $1.98 a gallon. Which *digit* in this price is represented by the *numeral* "9"?
(Answer: The *digit* in the tenths or "10 cents" position.)

Even or Odd?
If you take the decimal point out of $2.03, that makes the number 203. Is that an *even* or an *odd number*?
(Answer: *Odd*.)

Whole Numbers
Is $2.16 a *whole number*?
(Answer: No.)

Positive and Negative Numbers
To reinforce the difference between *positive* and *negative numbers*, have your student subtract the premium price from the regular price, and vice versa. For example:

If you subtract $2.13 (premium) from $1.89 (regular), what do you get? Is that a *positive* or *negative number*?
(Answers: -24 cents; *negative number*.)

Symbols

It's important for your student to get comfortable with the different kinds of numbers. He should add them, subtract them, multiply them, divide them, group them, list them in order, etc. Once your student can do these things, he can progress to the next exciting stage in math—conceptual thinking!

Instead of using numbers that "are there" to get an answer, your student needs to realize that **symbols** can **represent** numbers, and have meanings all their own.

THE GREAT UNKNOWNS

Luckily, symbols aren't confined to math problems. They appear in real life all of the time. So, of course, that's where we will go to improve your student's understanding of these words!

Symbol
Symbols are everywhere. They are basically shorthand for words and phrases, kind of like the hieroglyphs used by the ancient Egyptians. Work with your student to come up with ten common *symbols* you see in everyday life. They can be logos for TV networks or sports teams; *symbols* used to denote money; the ™ that stands for a trade-mark—anything that uses a *symbol* to stand for something else.

Represent
Once you have collected a group of *symbols*, have your student re-draw them and write a sentence explaining what each one *represents*. Make sure he uses the word "represents" in his sentence. For example:
> The symbol 🐏 *represents* Dodge trucks. It's a ram and means a Dodge is as tough as a ram.
> The symbol 🛡 *represents* Superman. It's the logo he has on his costume.

Variable
Have your student pick three easy-to-draw *symbols*. Now write three math problems for each *symbol* (that makes nine total), using the *symbols* as *variables* in the problem. For example:

$$3 + 🛡 + 4 = 9$$

What does the *variable* 🛡 *represent* in this problem?
(Answer: The number 2. 3 + 2 + 4 = 9.)

Do this one *symbol* at a time. By working with *symbols* your student already knows, she will learn that *symbols* (like 🛡 and 🐏 and like *x* and *y*) can mean anything you want them to mean in a math problem. They are *variables*.

WhizTip
Make teaching your student different symbols a part of your everyday life. Whenever you see a symbol, ask him what it means, and why. Variables become even more important in middle school.

Math

Lines

The ability to define which way a line "points"—**horizontal, vertical, diagonal**—or how two lines are related to each other —**parallel, perpendicular, intersect**—is important on elementary school math tests.

When I think of how lines **intersect**, I think of Bart Simpson riding his skateboard through Springfield as the credits roll on *The Simpsons* TV show. If you drew his route on a map, you would have all kinds of lines.

TRAVEL MAPS

Ask your student to think about where she goes on her wheels. Most kids these days have either a skateboard, rollerblades, scooter, or bicycle. (My mom never even learned how to ride a bicycle, but that's another story.)

Have your student draw a simple map of her journey the last time she used her favorite mode of transportation. If she can't remember the last time—tell her to get some fresh air! Then have her draw the diagram showing where she went. Here is mine from my bike ride yesterday.

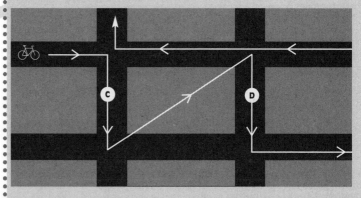

WhizTip

If your student isn't up to going on a bike ride, you can have her draw a diagram of any kind of activity—like walking around a grocery store, or riding the bus to school.

Now label some of the lines she drew and write three questions about the map she gives you, using the words above. Here's a sample question my mom wrote about my map:

How are lines C and D related to each other?
A. The are *perpendicular*.
B. They are *parallel*.
C. They *intersect*.
D. They are *diagonal*.

Answer: B.

Math

Polygons

A **polygon** is a shape with three or more flat sides. **Polygons** range from the familiar **triangle** to the exotic **rhombus**!

There are a ton of them, and some overlap. For instance, a square is a **rectangle**, but a **rectangle** isn't necessarily a square. An **octagon** is always a **polygon**, but a **polygon** isn't necessarily an **octagon**.

If you think it's confusing now, imagine if you were twenty minutes into a math test and you had to answer a question about them!

On the MCAS
Which two shapes below can you use to make the triangle shown?

CAR SHAPE GAME

No, it's not about the shapes of cars, it's a shape game you can play when you're in the car. But this one could end up costing you.

The next time you and your student are in the car together, take the change out of your pocket or change holder and put it on the dashboard tray or in the cup holder. Start calling out geometric shapes. Tell your student to find a real-world example of the shape. For every one he gets right, he gets a coin.

Start with something easy, like *octagon*. All stop signs are *octagons*. Go on to *triangle*, *rectangle*, *trapezoid*, etc. Tell him to look for the shapes in street signs, architecture, windows, and billboards. You probably won't be able to see them all on a normal drive, but if you play the game often, you will definitely end up a few dollars poorer, and your student will know his *polygons* much better.

The thing is, even if your student gets one wrong, or he just can't find a *quadrilateral*, he is still thinking and trying to figure out the shapes he sees. For example, you may call out "*equilateral triangle!*" and he may try to get away with an *isosceles triangle*. Use this occasion as an opportunity to discuss the difference.

<u>Note:</u> Want to spice it up a bit? Do "double or nothing" and have him define the shape after he has correctly spotted it. (This exercise is especially effective when a friend is also in the car providing some healthy competition.)

WhizWord
two-dimensional—adj.
All polygons are two-dimensional.
They have height and width.

Math

Angles

It is not enough to know what an angle is. It is also important to know many of the different types of angles. The thing is, the words used to describe them are NOT everyday words. Terms like **obtuse** and **congruent** are enough to frighten any student.

To get your student to think outside of traditional "math angles," you can use something way different than math class—a game that inspires fear in even the bravest of children.

Dodge ball.

What kid doesn't worry about the game of dodge ball? If she's not thinking about pegging an archenemy or a big-talking friend, she is thinking about evading the same people as they try to peg her themselves. And as everyone knows, dodge ball is all a game of angles.

DODGE BALL DIAGRAMS
Get paper and pencil. Have your student diagram scenes from a dodge ball game. It can be a real or an imagined game. It can be the throw of a ball and the direction it bounced off someone's rear end. It can be a particular evasion tactic. Just make sure she draws the angles of the actions in question, like so:

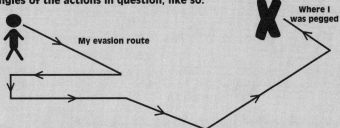

My evasion route

Where I was pegged

Now, ask her to label the angles *obtuse, acute, right,* and *congruent.* Just make sure she covers all of the angles listed above. After the first diagram, if she has drawn all *obtuse angles*, ask her to diagram a dodge ball move with *acute angles, congruent angles,* etc. Make sure she uses and labels each of the angles at least twice.

History and Social Science

Economics

The United States has a capitalist **economic** system. That means individuals own property, they produce **goods** and **services** at their jobs, and they are **consumers** of **goods** and **services**, too. The companies and individuals who are the **producers** of the **goods** and **services** try to make a **profit**.

Pretty dry stuff for a grade schooler. A good way to reinforce these words is to take an in-depth look at a company that makes a product your student can't get enough of. For instance—I just love Fruity Pebbles cereal. It tastes great and gives me the sugar rush I need to start the day out right.

WhizWord

supply and demand—n. When demand goes up, supply has to go up, too, or things get more expensive.

WORKING FOR A LIVING

For this exercise, your student needs to pick out a product he really gets a kick out of. It can be Fruity Pebbles, a magazine, a video game, a bicycle—anything he wants. Once he has chosen a product, you are going to ask him to write five short descriptions using the "Economics" words in relationship to the product. I will use Fruity Pebbles as an example:

- Describe a *consumer* of Fruity Pebbles.
- Describe the *producer* of Fruity Pebbles.
- Imagine what it would be like to be a worker in the breakfast cereal *industry*. What would your workday be like?
- What types of *goods and services* would the *producers* of Fruity Pebbles need to purchase to manufacture and sell their *product*?
- If you owned Fruity Pebbles, what would you do to make the company more *profits*?

If you want, you can have your student look up the company on the Internet to find some basic information—including the number of employees and its *profits* for the previous year or quarter.

You can also get more specific within each section. For example, for the *consumer* description, you can have him write down three characteristics that Fruity Pebbles *consumers* share, such as:

1. A love of breakfast cereal
2. A distaste for Count Chocula
3. High sugar tolerance

This is a fun exercise if you work on it together. Take your time and help your student with these new words. When you are done, if you think he could still use more work on them, repeat the exercise, but this time, you pick the company, and have your student help you write the answers.

History and Social Science
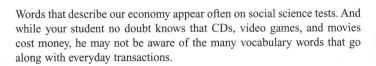

Markets and Trade

WhizWords

import—v.; n.
export—v.; n.
**I bet your student
has toys and
games, and I bet
they have labels
saying where they
were made. On a
regular basis, ask
him if a toy is an**
import **(yes/no),
and from what
country it was**
exported.

Words that describe our economy appear often on social science tests. And while your student no doubt knows that CDs, video games, and movies cost money, he may not be aware of the many vocabulary words that go along with everyday transactions.

A good way to help him nail down "Markets and Trade" words is to link them to how he takes part in markets and **trade** himself. For example, for the last year I have been washing cars for extra money. It's not glamorous, but it pays great. Anything your student does, or can do, to make money—babysitting, washing cars, selling cookies—will do. What you want him to do for this exercise is to think of his jobs or chores as a business partnership with you. I'll use washing cars as my example.

BE PARTNERS IN GRIME

Get out that pencil and paper. The most important part of a business partnership is figuring out a name. I call my urban car-washing company "Red's Wash-a-Matic." Write the partnership name at the top of your page.

Now write down the things your student will need to get started. I need:

- paper towels
- rags
- spray cleaner
- rubber cleaner

This is where you get involved. Bargain, *barter*, and *trade* with your student for the stuff she needs to get started. For example, I need a lot of Formula 409 to clean the outside of a car (two bottles), so I *trade* one extra night of doing dishes in exchange for a bottle of the stuff.

Make a list of the money and/or goods and services you have provided. For the things you have *purchased* for her, she will be in *debt*. Put a figure on that *debt*, either in dollars or in services (washing dishes). Once the business starts, she will have *income* that she can *credit* against that *debt*.

After you have shaken hands on the partnership, have her write a short business plan, using all the "Markets and Trade" words, just like any business partner would do.

Note: After she makes some money, take twenty percent of your student's *income*. Tell her that's the *tax* she has to pay for living under your roof. (Then give it back—you're just making a point!)

History and Social Science

War

Your student will learn a lot about wars in her history classes. Most of the class time is spent on the Revolutionary War and the Civil War, with a little bit on World Wars I and II thrown in.

So it's not a surprise that "War" words show up all the time on history tests. Some kids—like my friend Larry—eat this stuff up. Larry can rattle off the generals in all the big Civil War battles. But students like me, with other interests like sports and girls, can have a harder time of it. So a good way to get the words to stick in our heads is to put them on something we all understand—a poster!

Posters aren't just for rock stars and sports heroes. Historically, many nations have used **propaganda** posters to rally their citizens behind their war efforts. The World War II poster featuring Rosie the Riveter is probably the most famous **propaganda** poster, but posters have been a big part of fighting wars for years and years.

WhizTip

Your student's propaganda poster doesn't have to be about a war. It can be about anything she feels strongly about.

DESIGN A PROPAGANDA POSTER

Have your student create a poster for a conflict—it can be any war—using at least three of the words above. Underline the words. Here's one I did for the War Against Terrorism.

NEVER SURRENDER

The September 2001 attacks against our country make a strong national <u>defense</u> more important than ever.

Kids can help by <u>volunteering</u> and strengthening their communities, because real <u>patriotism</u> means a lot more than just waving flags.

Now, there are a ton of "War" words, so he probably won't be able to fit them all on one poster. Have him do two or three posters or flyers, then pick the one he likes best. Display that one on his bedroom wall or somewhere else in the house where he will see it every day.

Words Covered

checks and balances, Constitution, democracy, election, executive branch, House of Representatives, judicial branch, liberty, Senate

History and Social Science

Government

WhizTip

Have your student check her constitution **against the** Constitution **of the United States. See how her country's** elections, checks and balances **and** rights **and** responsibilities **compare.**

As the 2000 presidential **election** proved, our system of government is a complicated one based on **checks and balances**. The two guys gunning to be top dog of the **executive branch**, Bush and Gore, had to fight in the Florida's legislative and **judicial branches**, plus the **judicial branch** of the United States.

Of course, it would be a lot easier if we lived under a monarchy and all we had to remember was "the king is always right, and what he says goes." But then we wouldn't have all these cool unalienable rights to do whatever we want, like watch golf highlights on Sports Center at three o'clock in the morning. (See the "Citizenship" exercise for more on this.)

WRITE YOUR CONSTITUTION

Get a pencil and paper. Have your student name a country after herself. Now have her create her own *constitution* for a *democracy*, covering these three important parts of *democracy*: *elections* and how the government is structured.

Preamble
Write a short summary of your *constitution* (you may want to do this last).

Government
Cover the government using these words:
- *checks and balances*
- *Senate*
- *House of Representatives*
- *executive branch*
- *judicial branch*

Elections
Cover *elections* using these words:
- *democracy*
- *election*

Note: This is a hard exercise, so spend time with your student working on it. This exercise works best with both of you working together. To keep the fantasy going, ask her to appoint you as the vice president in her new country.

History and Social Science

Heritage

As you know, America is a country of **immigrants**. Only a small number of people can claim to descend from **native** peoples of this land. This makes words about **immigration** and different **customs** an important part of your student's education, because they are words about our country's history—especially in Boston.

The best way to introduce your student to these important vocabulary words is to focus on **immigrants** she is familiar with, including famous singers, athletes, and actors.

PROFILE A FAMOUS IMMIGRANT

Have your student write a short biography of someone he is interested in who immigrated from another country. Have him structure the story with the following headlines, using the following words under each headline:

> Celebrity name (short description)
> Home country (*majority, minority*)
> Customs of home country (*culture, custom, tradition*)
> Why did the celebrity come to the U.S.? (*migration*)

For example, one of my favorite singers of all time is Gloria Estefan. She had a bunch of hits with the Miami Sound Machine, and if it weren't for a terrible bus accident that sidelined her for a while, she would be bigger than Jennifer Lopez! Anyway, here's her story.

Celebrity Name
Gloria Estefan is a pop singer. She was born September 1, 1957. Called the "Queen of Latin Pop," Estefan has sold over 45 million records.

Home Country
Gloria is from Havana, Cuba. When she lived there, she was part of the Cuban *majority*. In the United States, Cuban immigrants are a *minority*.

Customs in Cuba
Some *customs* in Cuba are smoking big cigars and dancing to Cuban music. Cubans have a *traditional* music I learned about from a musical documentary called *The Buena Vista Social Club*. That *traditional* music is part of their *culture*.

Why She Came to the U.S.
Gloria escaped with her family two years after Fidel Castro took over the country. They *migrated* because they knew Castro would take away all of their freedoms.

WhizWord
persecute—v.
Immigrants and minorities are often persecuted in their new land. Persecute means to treat someone very badly, usually because of their race or religion.

WhizTip
There's a great immigration museum in Boston called Dreams of Freedom. For information on planning a visit, go to www.dreamsoffreedom.org.

Words Covered

boundary, climate,
continent, country, desert, equator,
fertile, geography, grassland,
hemisphere, latitude, legend, longitude,
pole, prime meridian, region, wetland

History and Social Science

Geography

WhizTip

Use this exercise in conjunction with the "Government" exercise to see how people and places interrelate. Have your student describe how his government would likely fare on his new continent.

These days, the world is a global village. That means no matter where you live, people on the other **continents** are your neighbors. It's mainly because transportation (planes and ships) and technology (satellites and the Internet) are so advanced, you can get from one **continent** to another faster than it used to take to get from one state to another!

But wouldn't it be nice if the global village got a new neighbor? I mean, two-thirds of the earth is covered by water—even more if global warming keeps melting the polar ice caps. Along with the problems of overpopulation, this means one thing—we need another **continent**! I think putting one smack dab in the middle of the Pacific Ocean would be great.

CREATING THE EIGHTH CONTINENT

For this exercise, your student will be imagining what the eighth continent will look like. Graph paper is best for this exercise, but any paper will do. First, have your student draw a BIG oval with an *equator* line across the middle. Mark the directions North, South, East, and West. That's the globe. Second, have her draw her *continent's* outline and name it. Third, have her draw different *regions* on her *continent*. Fourth, using the "Geography" words, have her create a *legend* for the different *regions*. Here is an example of my *continent* in the middle of the Pacific Ocean. I have named it "Redland."

Redland: The Eighth Continent

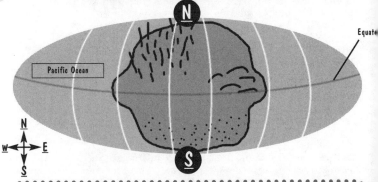

LEGEND

Grassland

Pole

Desert

Wetland

Once your student is done *continent*-building, have her write a short story about how its *geography* is similar to or different from our continent's *geography*, using at least three of the "Geography" words. For example: The *grasslands* just north of Redland's *equator* remind me of the *grasslands* in the Great Basin states I read about in *National Geographic*.

History and Social Science

Rebellion

The United States began with a **revolution** and hasn't looked back. Revolt—both peaceful and violent—has marked our country's history since it declared its **freedom** from England. And of course Massachusetts is synonymous with the **protests** and revolts that led to our break from England. Something called the Boston Tea Party comes to mind....

Anyway, when you are watching, reading, or listening to the news with your student, make sure you point out **revolutions**, large and small, going on around the country and the world. Explain the unfamiliar vocabulary words used in these stories to your student. He will undoubtedly come across these words in history class sooner or later.

YOUTHFUL REBELLIONS

Have your student organize a peaceful rebellion against something he thinks is unfair. Washing the dishes, bad cafeteria food, mowing the lawn, taking care of a younger sibling—you name it.

In order to gain support for his cause, he needs to create a *petition* explaining why he is doing what he is doing. He must use—and underline—all of the words above in his *petition* (this is kind of like the poster exercise we used for the "War" words). If he gets enough signatures, why not grant him his wish?

Here is part of a *petition* I put together asking my fellow Americans to boycott Jim Carrey movies until my dad lets me see them. Luckily, my dad was a good sport about it. I got forty-three signatures, so he let me watch *Dumb and Dumber*.

SIGN THE PETITION!

Red Schox begs you to sign this petition protesting the oppression by his father, Fred, who won't let Red watch Jim Carrey movies!

WhizTip

What revolt or revolution **does your student know the most about? The civil rights revolts of the 1960s? The American Revolution? Find out and compare notes.**

WhizWord

justice—**n. People organize** protests **and** boycotts **in an attempt to achieve** justice.

Social Studies

Community

WhizTip

Use this exercise along with the "Citizenship" exercise to help build a unified understanding of the words used to describe where and how we live as inhabitants of the United States.

I have lived in two different places so far in my life. I lived on North Captiva Island, a tiny little spot in the Lee Islands on the Gulf Coast, until I was six, and now I live in Boston, Massachusetts, by far the biggest city in the state, and one of the biggest cities in the country. I really like both of these **communities,** but for totally different reasons.

North Captiva is a **rural** community. It was separated from Captiva by huge storms and is now primarily state-owned land with a few houses and restaurants. It was really fun growing up there, a very pastoral lifestyle. It was just me and my sister and my parents most of the time. We never had much to do or anywhere special to go—it was like having free time all of the time. I got to be a great body surfer.

Boston is completely different. It is the quintessential **urban** community, with a bustling downtown area full of office buildings, a big international airport (Logan), basketball and baseball stadiums (Fleet Center and Fenway Park), and scores of colleges and universities, including my personal favorite, Boston University. Like I said, Boston is one of the United States's biggest cities, with a **population** of over half a million people. With so many people of every race, religion, and ethnic group, it's important everyone work to **coexist** as peacefully as possible.

DESCRIBE YOUR COMMUNITY
For this exercise, your student is going to describe the *community* she lives in. First, have her read the short descriptions of the two towns I have lived in (above), so she gets the hang of it. Then grab a pencil and paper and write the eight "Community" words at the top.

Now have her write a short paragraph describing your town. If it has *urban*, *rural*, and *suburban* sections, make sure she describes each of them. If it is all one type of *community*, have her describe why it is NOT the other two words. You want to make sure she knows the differences and similarities between them.

Note: If she is having trouble getting started, have your student write about her favorite thing to do in your town and her least favorite part of your town. That usually gets the creative juices flowing.

History and Social Science
Citizenship

A few years ago I just kind of thought of myself as a Schox. Perfect son of Fred and Ginger, little brother of Rose. But I've been learning in school that we are all **citizens** of the United States and important members of our local communities. My teachers keep explaining that we have **rights**—things no one can take away—and **responsibilities**—like obeying traffic signs and not littering.

The more I think about it, being a **citizen** is really just like being a member of a really, really big family.

WhizWord
respect—v.
Citizens **of Boston** must **respect** people's differences, **because our city is made up of people from so many different places.**

FAMILY CITIZEN

For this exercise, you are going to have your student describe what it means to be a good *citizen*—of your family. Families have rules and *responsibilities* a lot like communities do. So get a pencil and paper and have your student write down the following:

Rights	Responsibilities
1.	1.
2.	2.
3.	3.

Have him write at least three examples under each header. Work with him on the lists, talking about the difference between *rights* and *responsibilities*. Here are two examples from my Schox Family List:

The Schox Family R & R List

Rights	Responsibilities
1. Eat three tasty meals a day	1. Take out the trash on Tuesdays, Thursdays, and Saturdays

When you are done, have him compare being a *citizen* of your family to being a *citizen* of the United States. What are the similarities and differences in the *rights* and *responsibilities* for the two different communities? What *allegiances* does he have to his family? To his country?

Social Studies

Exploration

WhizWord

compass—n.
Explorers on
both land and
sea use a
compass to
navigate
uncharted
territories.

America's history is marked over and over again by **discovery** and **exploration**. From Christopher Columbus sailing from Spain to what he thought was India, to the westward expansion of American settlers, to astronauts poking around in outer space, our culture has always been obsessed with seeing what is on the other side.

So, many tests include questions about **discovery** and **exploration**. You don't want your student stumbling over "Exploration" words as she searches for the right answers, do ya? I thought not. Now, most of these words are pretty easy, so I am going to suggest a really fun exercise that will challenge your student's imagination as she learns the words.

WRITE A CLIFFHANGER

Have your student write a serialized story about *discovering* a new land. Have him end each story with a cliffhanger—an event that happens right at the end of the chapter that makes you want to turn the page. Use the "Exploration" words in the title of each chapter, in this order.

Chapter 1: Explore
Chapter 2: Navigate
Chapter 3: Discover
Chapter 4: Settler
Chapter 5: Colony

For example, the first chapter of my story is called "Nomar Garciaparra *Explores* Shortstop Beach." The last paragraph has him choosing between entering a dark cave to look for a magic talking baseball mitt OR taking advantage of some prime tanning hours on the beach. (Hint: He chooses the cave.)

Science

Biology

Did you know that a species of yellow moths turned gray when a coal-burning factory moved nearby? And it wasn't because they were covered with soot—it was because they needed to blend into their surroundings. When their surroundings were covered in soot, the moths that looked most like soot were able to hide from the birds. The others got eaten. In just a few years, all the yellow moths got eaten and became **extinct**, and the gray moths lived and **reproduced**.

It's called "natural selection" and "survival of the fittest." I learned it in biology class. Your student will need to know words like **inherited** and **generation** and **traits** in order to understand these concepts.

WhizTip

Is your student especially interested in a particular kind of animal or dinosaur? Have him write a short essay tracing its lineage.

IF TWO CELEBRITIES HAD A KID

Have you ever seen those "separated at birth" features in magazines and newspapers, where they show two celebrities who look almost identical? The funniest one I've ever seen is where they show Mick Jagger from the Rolling Stones and Barney Fife from *The Andy Griffith Show* right next to each other—and you cannot tell the difference. They look exactly the same. It is so funny.

Well, this exercise is similar, except we are going to imagine what *traits* a child of two celebrities would have. Buy a celebrity magazine—*People, InStyle,* and *Entertainment Weekly* have literally hundreds of celebrity photos. Have your student cut out pictures of two celebrities. Encourage him to find two celebrities who are more different than they are alike. For instance, I cut these two faces out of my dad's issue of *People*: the tall, low-voiced singer/actress Cher and the short, annoying-voiced actor/comedian Billy Crystal.

Now use the words above to describe their kid, and then write how these *traits* will help the kid survive (or become *extinct!*) in Hollywood.

Science and Technology/Engineering

Ecosystems

WhizTip

One great way to nail down these "Ecosystems" words is to visit a natural history museum. Bring this book with you and point out examples of each word.

When I think of an **ecosystem,** I think of a tropical rainforest, with lizards jumping after flying bugs, weird frogs **camouflaged** against tree trunks, huge ferns and flowers feeding off of **decomposing** plant life, and big palm trees, all dripping with water. Now that's an **ecosystem!**

But **ecosystems** don't have to be this dramatic. My family has a tiny back yard behind our house, and there are still a ton of **organisms** interacting back there. We get sparrows that eat the snails that eat the moss (a short **food web**). Lots of flowers that my dad plants end up getting eaten by aphids, and weeds that grow as tall as small trees hide the chain-link fence that surrounds our little **habitat.**

ECOSYSTEMS AROUND YOUR HOME

For this exercise your student is going to describe an *ecosystem* that exists near, around—or even in—your home. To start, get a pencil and paper. Have her pick an *ecosystem*—that's a system where different *organisms* all interact with each other. It can be a back yard, a nearby field, or woods. It can also be as small as a flower box or even the inside of an apartment.

Have her list the different *organisms* in the *ecosystem:* deer, flowers, possums, pine trees, grass, flies, mosquitoes, bluebirds, mice, cats, sisters, brothers, etc. When she's done making her list (five to fifteen *organisms* will do) have her write a story about how the *organisms* interact with each other, using the "Ecosystems" words.

When she's done, have her read it to you and then ask her questions about the *ecosystem* she picked. If some things don't make sense, work on her story with her until there is a final version she can keep and reread to brush up on these words. It doesn't have to win the Pulitzer, it just has to include all of the "Ecosystems" words and use them correctly.

Science

Geology

An eighteenth century gentleman farmer named James Hutton figured out the rock cycle. Rocks start out as molten lava that either explodes out of a volcano or stays trapped beneath the Earth's surface. Eventually, it cools and forms **igneous rock** (lava rock). Basalt and granite are common forms of **igneous rock**.

That **igneous rock** then goes through a lot of wear and tear. If it gets exposed to the elements on the Earth's surface, it breaks up and turns into stones and gravel and dust. That gets mixed and compacted with other bits and pebbles and forms **sedimentary rock**, like limestone and sandstone.

If **igneous** and **sedimentary rock** are reheated and exposed to immense pressure, they get squished into **metamorphic rock**, like marble.

WhizWord

texture—n.
**Different kinds
of rocks have
different** textures.
Igneous rocks
have a lumpy
texture,
sedimentary rocks
are rough, and
metamorphic
rocks **have a**
smooth texture.

LOCAL ROCK WALK

For this exercise you'll need a pencil and paper. Your student is going to create a Rock Walk Tour.

Work with your student to identify the three different rock types in or around your home and neighborhood. Be sure to consider the rocks that your home is actually made of, the stones in the yard, and any exposed rocks in nearby parks or open areas. As you go along, have your student make a map numbering and identifying the rocks on her rock walk. Here's part of a map that I made.

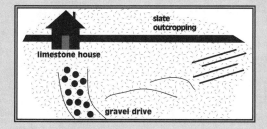

Once your student has completed her map, have her give a tour for friends and family. Your student plays the role of the Rock Walk Tour guide, identifying and explaining the different rocks and how they got that way.

Words Covered

biodegradeable, conservation, ecology, endangered, environment, erosion, habitat, life cycle, natural resources, organism, recycle, renewable, waste

Science and Technology/Engineering
The Environment

WhizTip

The best way to reinforce words is to to use them every day. Get your child involved in a volunteer program protecting natural resources in Massachusetts.

If kids ran the world, there wouldn't be such problems with the **environment**. We are natural **environmentalists**. For example, my school does that "Adopt-a-Highway" program—we've got three miles on the Interstate where we pick up trash twice a year. I also volunteer at the local animal shelter cleaning out cages, and when my dad sets mouse traps, I disable them.

Still, even though most kids care more than their parents about protecting the Earth, they don't necessarily understand the words that tests use to describe the **environment**.

ENVIRONMENTAL SUPERHERO

Most kids like comic books. So in this exercise, your student will be creating an *environmental* superhero—the defender of the ecosystem! Now, this isn't a new idea. That nature-loving super-hero Captain Planet had a comic book and a show on cable. (You can go to *www.turner.com/planet* to see what I'm talking about.) Your student may even have better ideas for an *environmental* superhero.

The first thing to do is pick out a name. I named my superhero "Habitattoo." He is covered in tattoos about *habitats* and the *environment*. His favorite one is the *recycling* symbol on his chest. Anyway, have your student create a superhero, and use the words above to say what this superhero does. You know—like Superman is "faster than a speeding bullet" and "able to leap tall buildings in a single bound." Habitattoo "protects *endangered species* with the strength of professional wrestler" and "*recycles* more plastic bottles than a chain of grocery stores."

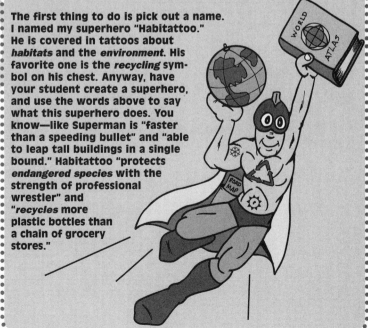

Science and Technology/Engineering
The Universe

People are obsessed with what is "out there." The *Star Wars* movies, the *Star Trek* TV series, the Space Shuttle, and the International Space Station all prove it. Let's face it—the universe is cool. If it wasn't, there wouldn't be countless television shows and movies about it, and we wouldn't be spending billions of dollars to explore it. So, not surprisingly, space and the universe play a big part on elementary school tests.

But don't get sucked into thinking that just because space is so popular, your student understands all the space vocabulary words. Give him the list of "The Universe" words above and ask him if he's familiar with them. If he knows them, great, watch the *Star Wars* trilogy on DVD together and move on. If not, let's keep playing make believe.

WhizTip

If you have cable, watch the Discovery Channel with your student. If you don't, get out your *TV Guide* and watch for PBS documentaries about space.

SAVE US SUPERHERO, SAVE US!

In the previous exercise, your student created a superhero who defends the environment. Now, have her write and/or draw a short comic strip where the character goes to another planet to save its environment. Use one word from the list above in each cell. One way for you to get more involved is for your student to write the strip and for you to draw it, or vice versa.

Here are the first two cells of a comic strip where my superhero, Habitattoo, goes to Saturn to save its rings from spinning out of control and smashing into neighboring Jupiter.

Word Whiz

Vocabulary Lists

This is not a dictionary! It's a list of 525 words that are important for grade school students to know. All of the words in the book's exercises are listed back here, along with other words your student should know when:

- **doing homework assignments**
- **taking tests at school**
- **preparing for and taking standardized tests**

All of these words should become part of your student's vocabulary.

I have written one or two "everyday" definitions for each word, along with sample sentences and illustrations here and there for the toughest ones.

If your student—or you!—needs pronunciation help or a more complete definition for a word, use a dictionary.

Word Whiz List
Test Instructions

after *adv.*—following something in a series. The opposite of *before*.

approximately *adv.*—close, but not exactly.

before *adv.*—previous to something in a series. The opposite of *after*.

best *adj.*—in test instructions, <u>best</u> is used all of the time. "<u>Best</u> answer" means the answer that makes the most sense; "<u>best</u> judgment" means use your common sense; etc. *Example:* What is the <u>best</u> estimate of the depth of the lake?

between *adv.*—in the middle of two other things.

clue *n.*—piece of evidence; hint.

common *adj.*—shared; belonging to more than one. *Example:* Which hair color is most <u>common</u>?

compute *v.*—to calculate. *Example:* <u>Compute</u> 65 multiplied by 6.

correct *adj.*—right. *Example:* Write the <u>correct</u> number in each circle above.

decrease *v.*—to lessen. *Example:* If you <u>decrease</u> an amount, it becomes smaller.

difference *n.*—the remainder; the amount left when you subtract one number from another. *Example:* Find the <u>difference</u> between these two quantities.

estimate *n.*—an approximation. *Example:* What is the best <u>estimate</u> of the total number of hot dogs eaten at a typical Red Sox game?

evidence *n.*—proof. *Example:* Using <u>evidence</u> from the story, explain how Tom came to be class president.

example *n.*—occurrence. *Example*: Which of the following is an <u>example</u> of the story's setting?

explain *v.*—to make clear. *Example:* <u>Explain</u> the steps you used to find the answer.

fact *n.*—something that is definitely true. *Example*: In this story, which of these is a <u>fact</u>?

first *adj.*—number one; occurring before all others. The opposite of *last*.

following *v.*—being the next in a series.

greatest *adj.*—most. *Example:* What is the <u>greatest</u> number of bird houses you can make with these materials?

highest *adj.*—most (just like *greatest*); the uppermost. *Example:* What is the <u>highest</u> total she can get by throwing three darts?

identify *v.*—pick out. *Example:* <u>Identify</u> the parallelograms.

increase *v.*—to grow; to add to. *Example:* If you <u>increase</u> a quantity, it becomes larger.

italics *n.*—a word style where all the letters slant to the right. *Like this.*

last *adj.*—occurring after all others. The opposite of *first*.

least *adv.*— 1) lessermost. 2) *adj.* smallest in size.

likely *adj.*—probable. *Example:* What is the likely reason Carl saved the injured heron?

lowest *adj.*— least; lowermost. *Example:* What is the lowest elevation of the three mountains shown?

main *adj.*—most important; primary. *Example:* What is the main theme of Smyrna's speech?

mainly about *n.*—mostly about. *Example:* The first paragraph of the story gives information mainly about:

middle *n.*—the center. *Example:* Which line passes through the middle of the circle?

most *adj.*—1) greatest in number or size. 2) *adv.* to the highest degree.

most likely *adv.*—probably. *Example:* Which card is most likely next?

next *adj.*—following in a series. *Example:* What are the next three numbers in this number pattern?

opinion *n.*—what a person thinks, regardless of the facts. *Example:* It is my opinion that the New York Knicks have had the best team in the NBA for the last ten years, even though they haven't won a championship.

parentheses *n.*—these things: ( ). In English language arts, parentheses are used to set off a clause in a sentence. *Example:* I must go to the store (there is a sale on soap). In math, parentheses are used to set off groups of operations. *Example:* (3+4) (4-3) =.

possible *adj.*—capable of happening. *Example:* Which is NOT a possible outcome?

predict *v.*—to foretell; to deduce. *Example:* Based on the information in the paragraph, predict how Gus will react to the news his turtle won First Prize.

probably *adv.*—most likely. *Example:* What will Kevin probably do next, throw the fish back or eat it for dinner?

purpose *n.*—reason. *Example:* What is the purpose of the symbols inside the shapes?

reason *n.*—purpose *Example:* Give a reason why Louise's choice of sweater may have been unwise.

similar *adj.*—alike. *Example:* Which of the angles are similar?

sort *v.*—to categorize. *Example:* Sort the following figures into two groups.

specific *adj.*—exact. *Example:* Name four specific places Megan should look for jewelry.

true *adj.*—correct. *Example:* Which statement is true about the first Spaniards who arrived in South America?

unlikely *adj.*—probably not going to happen. *Example:* Is it unlikely that Ned will require stitches?

usually *adj.*—often; most of the time. *Example:* Does the writer usually make his characters mean or nice?

which *adj.*—what particular one. *Example:* Which statement is true about the first Spaniards who arrived in South America?

who, what, where, when, why *adj.*—the five answer clues! These words are clues to tip off test takers that a question involves a person (*who*), place (*where*), thing (*what*), time (*when*), or reason (*why*). (See the exercise on page 10 for more on this.)

Word Whiz List

English Language Arts

abbreviation *n.*—a shorter way of writing a word. *Example*: *Mr.* is an abbreviation of *Mister*.

adjective *n.*—a word that describes a noun or a pronoun. *Example*: That's a *dirty* dog.

adverb *n.*—a word that modifies a verb, adjective, or another adverb. *Example:* That's a *really* dirty dog.

alliteration *n.*—the use of a series of words with the same first letter. *Example:* Simply said, Simon was seriously sick.

antonym *n.*—the opposite of a word. *Example:* mean/nice.

author *n.*—someone who writes books, plays, speeches, or articles.

autobiography *n.*—a biography written by the person it's about.

biography *n.*—a story of someone's life.

capitalize *v.*—to make a letter uppercase. *Example:* ABC, not abc.

cause and effect *n.*—when something happens, there is a consequence. Think of one of those record-breaking domino set-ups. When you tip the first domino over (cause), the whole set-up goes haywire (effect).

character *n.*—a person in a book, play, movie, or TV show.

chronological *adj.*—arranged in order of when things occurred.

compare *v.*—to consider the similarities between things. On tests, compare is often used with *contrast*. *Example:* Compare and contrast the views of Writer A and Writer B.

complete sentence *n.*—a sentence made up of the proper parts of speech and punctuation. A complete sentence includes a subject (the topic of the sentence) and a predicate (the verb and its related words).

compound sentence *n.*— a sentence made up of two complete sentences, usually joined with a conjunction and/or a comma. *Example:* I researched the topic in the encyclopedia at school, but I ended up finding the information I needed online.

conclusion *n.*—end; answer. *Example:* At the story's conclusion, the writer reached the conclusion that crime does not pay.

conjunction *n.*—a word joining other words together in a sentence, such as *and*, *or*, *so*, and *but*. *Example*: Bob *and* Shanyce wanted cookies, *but* their dad gave them carrots instead.

conscience *n.*—something inside you that knows the difference between right and wrong.

consistent *adj.*—staying the same. *Example*: Omar Visquel is a consistent shortstop for the Cleveland Indians: he catches anything hit to him and

base almost every time.

consonant *n.*—a letter of the alphabet that isn't a vowel.

contraction *n.*—a shortened form of two words, usually using an apostrophe. *Examples:* are + not= aren't; that + is = that's; is + not = isn't.

contrast *v.*—to look at the differences between things. On tests, contrast is often used with *compare*. *Example:* Compare and contrast the views of Writer A and Writer B.

define *v.*—to explain. *Example:* I am doing my best to define the words students need to know to do well on the MCAS and other tests.

describe *v.*—to explain, using details.

detail *n.*—a small part of a bigger whole. On tests, students are often asked to find details in a piece of writing to support their answers.

dialogue *n.*—the speaking parts in a book, play, movie, or TV show.

draft *n.*—the first version of a piece of writing. *Example*: Jill wrote a draft of her essay, then corrected her spelling, punctuation, and grammar to create a final version.

edit *v.*—to revise or change a piece of writing to make it better.

essay *n.*—a piece of nonfiction writing that is usually expository or persuasive.

exclamation *n.*—something said strongly and loudly. In writing, an exclamation is expressed with an exclamation point!

fable *n.*—a story that uses characters to teach a lesson. *Example*: Aesop's Fables.

fact *n.*—something that really exists or really happened. On tests, it is often used with *opinion*. *Example*: Is the statement a fact or an opinion?

familiar *adj.*—1) common. 2) having a good understanding of.

fantasy *n.*—1) an imaginary story. 2) the opposite of reality.

fiction *n.*—1) a story someone creates using his or her imagination. *Example*: The *Harry Potter* books are works of fiction. 2) a lie or untruth. *Example:* Separating fact from fiction.

figurative *adj.*—using figures of speech. *Example:* I used figurative language in my essay when I said my dad was "cool as a cucumber." That's a figure of speech that means "calm."

folklore *n.*—stories handed down from generation to generation.

genre *n.*—style. *Example:* Fiction and nonfiction are two writing genres.

glossary *n.*—the section at the back of a book with definitions of words used in the book. (Basically, what you're reading right now!)

hero, heroine *n.*—the man (hero) or woman (heroine) who saves the day. *Example:* Many heroes and heroines risked their own lives to save others after terrorists destroyed the World Trade Center.

homonym *n.*—words that are spelled and pronounced alike, but have different meanings. *Example:* fry (to cook) and fry (a julienned potato).

homophone *n.*—words that are pronounced alike, but have different spellings and meanings. *Example:* way (direction) and weigh (to take the weight of).

illustrator *n.*—someone who draws the pictures that go along with a story.

imagery *n.*—the act of painting a picture (image) with words. *Example:* At the climbers' high altitude, the stars *glittered like diamonds.*

imaginary *adj.*—not real; "in your head."

incomplete sentence *n.*—a sentence that is missing one or more parts of speech.

indent *v.*—to set off the beginning of a paragraph with spaces.

index *n.*—the alphabetical list of a book's contents found in the back of a book.

influence *n.*—1) the power to affect an outcome. 2) *v.* to affect an outcome.

interpret *v.*—to explain the meaning of. *Example*: I interpreted the data from the science experiment to mean that the tree was 26 years old.

interrogative sentence *n.*—a question. In writing, an interrogative sentence is denoted by a question mark. Isn't it?

interview *n.*—a conversation in which one person asks all the questions and the other person answers them.

legend *n.*—1) the explanation of the symbols on a map. 2) *n.* a popular historical story.

legible *adj.*—readable. *Example*: Make sure your answers are legible.

limerick *n.*—a funny poem where lines 1, 2, and 5 rhyme with each other and lines 3 and 4 rhyme with each other.
Example: There once was a plumber named Ray
                        Who fixed seven toilets a day.
                        He came home one night
                        And found something not right.
                        His dog had run off with his pay.

metaphor *n.*—a figure of speech in which one thing is related to something else. *Example:* The actress' skin was *cashmere*, her eyes *two diamonds*, her lips *rolled-up $100 bills*.

moral *n.*—the lesson a story or fable gets across. *Example*: The moral of the story? Never turn your back on an angry bear.

myth *n.*—a story that explains the world or the universe. It usually involves gods, heroes, and adventures.

narrator *n.*—the teller of a story. *Example*: The narrator of the *Adventures of Sherlock Holmes* is Dr. Watson.

nonfiction *n.*—a true story.

noun *n.*—a word that names a person, place, or thing.

onomatopoeia *n.*—the use of words to imitate their meaning. *Examples*: *buzz* and *splat*.

opinion *n.*—what someone thinks about something.

opposite *n.*—something completely different than something else.

paraphrase *v.*—to restate using other words.

personification *n.*—the representation of a concept or a thing as a person. *Example*: Tiger Woods is the personification of good sportsmanship.

persuade *v.*—to convince.

plot *n.*—the events of a story.

plural *n.*—the form of a word that means "more than one." *Example*: The plural form of *gopher* is *gophers*.

poem *n.*—a composition in either rhyming or free verse (no rhymes).

point of view *n.*—one person's opinion or way of looking at things.

possessive *n.*—a form of a word that shows ownership. *Examples*: baker, *baker's* / me, *mine*.

prefix *n.*—a few letters added to the beginning of a word that change its meaning. *Example: dis-* (*dis*orderly), *ir-* (*ir*retrievable), and *de-* (*de*claw) are examples of prefixes.

preposition *n.*—a word that relates a noun or pronoun to another word or phrase. *Example*: Ronnie ran and got help *for* Keith when Keith got *in* trouble.

pronoun *n.*—a word that takes the place of a noun. *Examples*:

milk = *it*. Harold = *he* .

proper noun *n.*—the name of a specific person, place, or thing.

proverb *n.*—a common saying that tells a truth. *Example:* Give a man a fish and you feed him for a day. Teach a man to fish and you feed him for a lifetime.

punctuation *n.*—the parts of a sentence that aren't words. *Examples*: period, comma, question mark.

research *v.*—to study carefully. It usually involves going to the library or online to <u>research</u> information on a subject.

retell *v.*—repeat. *Example:* <u>Retell</u> in your own words the story of Britney Spears's rise to superstardom.

revise *v.*—to change to improve; to amend.

rhyme *v.*—to link words that sound alike. *Example*: On my morning jog I came across a dog and a frog sitting on a log in a bog in the fog.

root *n.*—a word or part of a word from which other words are formed. *Example:* <u>root</u> = *stink*. Words formed from *stink*: *stinker*, *stinky*.

run-on sentence *n.*—a sentence that continues on longer than it should, usually by using too many conjunctions.

scene *n.*—a small section of a movie, play, or TV show.

sequence *n.*—one thing following after another.

setting *n.*—the location and time in which a story takes place.

simile *n.*—a description that uses the words "like" or "as." *Example:* The actress's hair is *as soft as silk*.

singular *adj.*—relating to one of something.

suffix *n.*—a few letters added to the end of a word to change its meaning. *Examples*: –*ness* (bitter*ness*), -*ly* (like*ly*), and –*ion* (tens*ion*) are <u>suffixes</u>.

suggest *v.*—to offer for consideration.

summarize *v.*—to write a shorter version of a long piece of writing where you just cover the main points.

support *v.*—to give evidence proving or explaining something. *Example*: Please <u>support</u> your theory that girls are much better than boys.

syllable *n.*—one chunk of a word that makes up single sound. The <u>syllables</u> in <u>syllable</u> are *syl*, *la*, and *ble*.

synonym *n.*—a word that means about the same thing as another. *Examples*: *smart* and *intelligent*; *couch* and *sofa*; *road* and *street*.

table of contents *n.*—the list of chapters in the beginning of a book.

tall tale *n.*—an exaggerated story that isn't true. *Example:* My sister told a <u>tall tale</u> about how she got grass stains on her best pants. Her story involved both stampeding cattle and helping an old lady cross the street.

tense *n.*—the form of a verb that tells when the action takes place. *Example:* verb = love. <u>future tense</u> = will love; <u>past tense</u> = loved; <u>present tense</u> = love.

theme *n.*—the subject for a story. In school, students are often asked to write a story on a particular <u>theme</u>, such as "What did you do this summer?"

title *n.*—the name of a book, story, or other creative work.

verb *n.*—an action word. *Examples*: *run, spell, consider*.

visualize *v.*—to picture in your mind.

vowel *n.*—the letters that aren't consonants, namely a, e, i, o, and u (and sometimes y).

Word Whiz List

Math

acute angle *n.*—an angle less than 90°.

add *v.*—to combine two or more numbers. *Example*: 11 + 13 = 24.

addend *n.*—a number to be added to another number.

angle *n.*—the figure made where two straight lines meet.

area *n.*—the amount of space inside a triangle, rectangle, circle, etc.

associative *adj.*—when an operation works independent of how numbers are grouped. *Example:* (a + b) + c = a + (b + c).

average *n.*—the number you get by adding two or more numbers, then dividing by how many numbers you added up. *Example:* The <u>average</u> of the numbers 4, 6, 8, and 10 is 7. (4 + 6 + 8 + 10 = 28. 28 ÷ 4 = 7.)

axes *n.*—the plural form of axis. <u>Axes</u> are the horizontal and vertical lines that make up a graph. They are usually (but not always) named the *x*-axis and *y*-axis.

chance *n.*—the probability something will happen. *Example:* What is the <u>chance</u> Bill will make his next shot if he makes 3 out of every 5 shots?

circle *n.*—a perfectly round shape.

circumference *n.*—the length of the boundary of a circle.

combine *v.*—to add together.

commutative *n.*—independent of order. *Example:* 3 x 2 = 2 x 3.

cone *n.*—an object that has a circle as its base and tapers to a point.

congruent *adj.*—having the same shape (usually used to describe angles and triangles). *Example*: If you lay one <u>congruent</u> triangle on top of another, they match exactly.

cube *n.*—an object with six square faces, all the same size. *Example*: a sugar <u>cube</u>.

cubic *adj.*—having the volume of a cube with an edge of a stated length. *Example:* The volume of this box is 4 <u>cubic</u> feet.

cylinder *n.*—an object that has circles at its base and top.

data *n.*—the facts and figures in a math problem.

decimal *n.*—1) a different way to write a fraction. 2) the part after the period in a number. *Examples*: .<u>20</u>, 3.<u>45</u>, –10.<u>5</u>

decimal point *n.*—a period dividing whole numbers from parts of

four-sided figure.

diameter *n.*—the distance across the center of a circle.

digit *n.*—1, 2, 3, 4, 5, 6, 7, 8, 9, and 0 are <u>digits</u>.

distance *n.*—the measurement between two points or things.

divide *v.*—to calculate how many times one number goes into another number. Division problems often use the division symbol: ÷. *Example:* 4 ÷ 2 = 2.

dividend *v.*—a number to be divided by another; the number on the top in a fraction.

divisor *n.*—the number that is divided into the dividend.

double *v.*—to multiply by two.

dozen *n.*—a group of 12. *Example:* a <u>dozen</u> eggs.

equal *adj.*—the same.

equation *n.*—a "math sentence"; a math statement where two quantities are equal to each other. *Example:* 2 x 4 = 8.

equilateral triangle *n.*—a triangle with all three sides the same length.

equivalent *adj.*—the same.

estimate *v.*—1) to guess; to come as close as possible to the real answer. 2) *n.* an educated guess.

even number *n.*—a number that can be divided by two evenly (no remainder). *Examples:* 2, -4, 6, 18, -20, and 22 are all <u>even numbers</u>.

extend *v.*—to make longer or bigger; to continue. *Example:* <u>Extend</u> this number pattern three places: 2, 4, 8, 16, __, __, __.

factor *n.*—1) any of the numbers that can be multiplied together to get a product. *Example:* 2, 7, 14, and 1 are the <u>factors</u> of 14. 2) *v.* to break a number down into its factors.

factorial *n.*—the product of all of the positive integers leading up to and including a given number, commonly denoted with that number and an exclamation point (!). *Example:* 5! = 1 x 2 x 3 x 4 x 5.

fraction *n.*—1) two numbers with a line between them. 2) part of whole number. *Examples:* 1/2, 5/4, 1/6.

graph *n.*—1) a chart that shows number relationships, usually with an *x*-axis and a *y*-axis. 2) *v.* to chart number relationships.

height *n.*—how tall something is.

hexagon *n.*—a polygon with six sides.

horizontal *adj.*—going left to right (or right to left).

intersect *v.*—to cross. *Example:* When two streets cross each other, they <u>intersect</u>.

inverse *n.*—the reciprocal of a quantity. *Examples:* The <u>inverse</u> of 6 is 1/6. The <u>inverse</u> of 2/3 is 3/2.

isosceles triangle *n.*—a triangle with two sides of equal length.

length *n.*—the distance between a beginning and an end.

equilateral triangle

isosceles triangle

1/6. The <u>inverse</u> of 2/3 is 3/2.

isosceles triangle *n.*—a triangle with two sides of equal length.

length *n.*—the distance between a beginning and an end.

line segment *n.*—part of a line, usually marked with points.

mass *n.*—the size and the bulk of something.

mean *n.*—the average of a group of numbers. (See the definition of *average* for an example.)

median *n.*—the middle one in a group of numbers, so the same number of numbers are above and below it.

mixed number *n.*—a number made up of a whole number and a fraction. *Example:* 4 6/7.

mode *n.*—in a group of numbers, the one that occurs the most number of times.

multiple *n.*—a number that is the product of one number multiplied by a whole number, leaving no remainder. *Example*: <u>Multiples</u> of 5 are *5* (5 x 1); *10* (5 x 2); *15* (5 x 3); etc.

multiply *v.*—to add numbers together a bunch of times. *Example*: 3 x 5 means adding 3 to itself 5 times (3 + 3 + 3 + 3 + 3).

negative number *n.*—1) a number less than zero. 2) a number with a minus sign in front of it. *Examples*: –4, –23.3, –400, –.4, –3/4

net *adj.*—the final result. *Example:* What is the <u>net</u> amount of puppets left after the damaged puppets are taken away?

number sentence *n.*—a mathematical operation. *Example*: 8 + 4 = 12.

numeral *n.*—a symbol used for a quantity. *Examples*: 1, 2, and 3 are <u>numerals</u>. X, V, and I are Roman <u>numerals</u>.

numerator *n.*—the number on top in a fraction; the dividend.

obtuse angle *n.*—an angle great than 90°.

octagon *n.*—an eight-sided shape.

odd number *n.*—a number that, when divided by two, gives you a remainder. *Examples*: 1, 3, 5…19, 21, 23.

one-dimensional *adj.*—a measure in only one direction, such as length (but not width).

order *v.*—to arrange one after the other. *Example:* <u>Order</u> the farmer's harvests over the last five years from biggest to smallest.

organize *v.*—to arrange in order (see above).

pair *n.*—two of something. *Example*: a <u>pair</u> of shoes.

parallel *adj.*—two lines that never meet. *Example*: Train tracks are <u>parallel</u> to each other.

parallelogram *n.*—a four-sided figure with parallel opposite sides.

pattern *n.*—something repeating itself.

pentagon *n.*—a five-sided figure.

percent *n.*—per 100. *Example:* 20 is 20 <u>percent</u> of 100.

perfect square *n.*—a number with an integer for its square root.

pie chart, pie graph *n.*—a circular chart where the pieces stand for percentages. *Note*: It looks like a pizza.

place value *n.*—the position of a numeral in a number. *Example:* In the number 2,345, the place value of 2 is "thousands," the place value of 3 is "hundreds," the place value of 4 is "tens," and the place value of 5 is "ones."

plane *n.*—a flat surface. *Note*: Think of "the Great *Plains*."

polygon *n.*—a shape with three or more sides.

positive number *n.*—a number greater than zero.

prime number *n.*—a number that has only itself and one as factors. *Examples*: 17, 23, 101.

probability *n.*—the chance something will happen. *Example:* If you flip a coin, the probability that it will turn up tails is 1:2.

product *n.*—the answer to a multiplication problem.

pyramid *n.*—an object with triangles for its sides and a polygon for its base. *Note*: Think of the Great Pyramids of Egypt.

quadrilateral *n.*—a shape with four sides.

quotient *n.*—the answer to a division problem.

radius *n.*—the distance from the center to the edge of a circle.

random *adj.*—in no particular order.

range *n.*—the difference between the highest and lowest numbers in a group of numbers.

ratio *n.*—the relationship between two quantities. *Example*: 15 students per one teacher = 15:1 student/teacher ratio.

rectangle *n.*—a shape with four sides and four right angles. *Note*: Each set of parallel sides has the same length.

remainder *n.*—the number left over in a division problem.

represent *v.*—to take the place of. *Example*: In this problem, *q* represents the number 4.

result *n.*—answer.

rhombus *n.*—a polygon with four equal sides (but not necessarily four equal angles); an equilateral parallelogram.

right angle *n.*—a 90° angle. A right angle is formed when two lines intersect perpendicularly.

rotate *n.*—to turn on an axis.

round *adj.*—1) having no corners, like a circle. 2) *v.* to estimate by going up or down to the closest number. *Example*: If you are rounding to the nearest whole number, 6.75 rounds up to 7. If you are rounding down to the nearest tens place, 112 rounds down to 110.

scale *n.*—proportion. *Example:* I have a model of a Japanese Zero plane that is 1/8 the scale of a real one.

segment *n.*—part of a line, usually marked with points.

set *n.*—group. *Example:* Pick your answer from the following number sets.

quadrilaterals

radius

sphere *n.*—a round, ball-shaped object; an object with all points on its surface the same distance from its center.

square root *n.*—the number you multiply by itself to get a given value. *Example*: $2 = \sqrt{4}$ (because 2 x 2 = 4).

subtract *v.*—to take one number away from another. *Example*: $12 - 3 = 9$.

sum *n.*—the result of addition. *Example*: The <u>sum</u> of 4 + 5 is 9.

survey *n.*—a sampling of opinions.

symbol *n.*—something that stands for something else.

symmetry *n.*—sameness on each side of a dividing line.

three-dimensional *adj.*—having volume and depth. *Example*: A sphere is <u>three-dimensional</u>.

total *n.*—the result of addition; sum.

trapezoid *n.*—a quadrilateral with two parallel sides.

triangle *n.*—a three-sided figure.

two-dimensional *adj.*—on a single plane; having no volume. *Example*: A circle is <u>two-dimensional</u>.

unknown *n.*—quantity to be found. *Example:* Solve for the <u>unknown</u> n in this equation: $6n + 2 = 20$. $n = 3$

value *n.*—in math, an assigned number or numerical quantity.

variable *n.*—something with a value that can vary (change). In math, <u>variables</u> are usually called x and y.

Venn diagram *n.*—a diagram that uses circles to represent relationships among groups.

Venn Diagram

vertex *n.*—the point where two edges of a shape meet. The plural form of <u>vertex</u> is <u>vertices</u>.

vertical *adj.*—pointing straight up and down.

volume *n.*—the amount of space a three-dimensional object occupies.

weight *n.*—the measure of how heavy something is.

whole number *n.*—an integer; a number that is not a fraction or a decimal.

width *n.*—the distance from side to side; how wide something is.

History and Social Science

A.D. *adv.*—stands for "Anno Dominus." Also written sometimes as CE ("Common Era"). You count forward in "A.D. time," so <u>A.D.</u> 50 happened *before* <u>A.D.</u> 100. *Note:* <u>A.D.</u> precedes the year it identifies, but <u>B.C.</u> follows the year (see below).

adapt *v.*—to change to meet new circumstances.

agriculture *n.*—the act of growing crops and raising livestock. *Example:* An agrarian society revolves around <u>agriculture</u>.

allegiance *n.*—devotion to a person, group, or country.

amendment *n.*—a change that corrects or improves something. *Note*: Most often used in class and on tests in relation to <u>amendments</u> to the Constitution.

ammunition *n.*—bullets and bombs.

ancient *adj.*—really, really, really old. *Example:* On my trip to Egypt I visited the <u>ancient</u> tombs of the pharaohs.

artifact *n.*—an object from a period of time. *Example:* The tombs in Egypt are filled with <u>artifacts</u>, including gold statues and pretty vases.

assemble *v.* —to gather together.

barter *v.*—to pay for stuff with other stuff, instead of with money. *Example*: Fred <u>bartered</u> for the Persian rug. He ended up paying the merchant two chickens and a goat for it.

B.C. *adv.*—stands for "Before Christ." Also written sometimes as BCE ("Before the Common Era"). *Note:* You count backwards in "<u>B.C.</u> time," so 50 <u>B.C.</u> happened *after* 100 <u>B.C.</u>

benefit *n.*—something that helps.

boundary *n.*—a division between one area of land and another. *Example:* Which <u>boundary</u> do Country A and Country B share?

boycott *v.*—to refuse to buy something or do something in protest.

budget *n.*—the plan for how a country—or person—will spend its money.

canal *n.*—a man-made waterway that boats and barges use to carry stuff from place to place.

cash crop *n.*—a harvest that is sold on the market. *Example:* Which is Iowa's largest <u>cash crop</u>, corn or soybeans?

century *n.*—a period of 100 years. *Note*: The <u>century</u> is "one more" than the number. 1671 is part of the seventeenth century. 1945 is part of the twentieth century.

usually involves defined rights and responsibilities.

civilization *n.*—a group of people who have shown ability in language, agriculture, art, and commerce.

civil rights *n.*—rights due a person because he is a citizen of a country. *Note*: This term is often used in reference to minorities' struggles for civil rights.

climate *n.*—the weather of a particular region.

coexist *v.*—to live together. *Example:* Did the two tribes mentioned in the passage choose to go to war or to peacefully coexist?

colony *n.*—a civilization start-up. *Note*: This term is often used in reference to the European colonization of much of the globe in the 16th-19th centuries.

commerce *n.*—the buying and selling of goods and services.

communication *n.*—the act of exchanging information.

community *n.*—a group of people who share a common bond. They usually live in the same area, but communities can also revolve around interests and backgrounds.

compass *n.*—a device used to find direction.

conflict *n.*—fighting. *Example*: Human history is a history of conflict.

Congress *proper noun*—the U.S. Senate and House of Representatives. *Note*: Congress is one of the three branches of the U.S. government.

consequence *n.*—the result of an action.

conserve *v.*—to save by using sparingly. *Example*: Conserve energy.

Constitution *proper noun*—the rules around which the government of the United States was built. In general, a constitution is a document stating the laws and principals governing a nation, state, or organization.

consumer *n.*—a person who buy goods and services.

continent *n.*—one of the seven major land masses on Earth: Africa, Antarctica, Asia, Australia, Europe, North America, South America.

contribute *n.*—to give. *Example*: I went door-to-door asking neighbors to contribute canned goods to my school's Thanksgiving food drive.

cooperate *v.*—to work together.

country *n.*—nation; land where people live under the same government.

credit *n.*—a system where you buy something now but pay for it later. *Example:* My parents bought our washer and dryer on credit. They start making payments on them next year.

culture *n.*—a group of people bound by shared customs, laws, and beliefs.

custom *n.*—a tradition or behavior of a country's citizens.

debt *n.*—the amount of money owed to others. *Example:* My parents are $1,000 in debt to WasherTown. They owe them that much money for the washer and dryer they bought on credit.

decade *n.*—a period of ten years.

defense *n.*—the measures taken to protect something.

delegate *n.*—a representative; someone chosen to speak for others. *Example*: Elected officials are the delegates of the people.

democracy *n.*—a system of government based on the principle of equality where people hold the power.

delegate *n.*—a representative; someone chosen to speak for others. *Example*: Elected officials are the <u>delegates</u> of the people.

democracy *n.*—a system of government based on the principle of equality where people hold the power.

desert *n.*—1) a dry, hot, sandy area. 2) *v.* to leave.

discover *v.*—to find for the first time ever.

discrimination *n.*—the treatment of some people worse than others without a good reason. (See the definition for *prejudice*.)

diversity *n.*—in social science, it's a situation where there are a lot of different kinds of people—different colors, religions, incomes, and backgrounds—all living together.

domestic *adj.*—having to do with one's home or one's country. *Example*: Presidents have to deal with problems both foreign and <u>domestic</u>.

economy *n.*—the way a country or community manages its resources. *Note*: In a market <u>economy</u>, private citizens own the means of production (companies, factories, and farms).

election *n.*—the casting of votes to choose among candidates.

equator *n.*—an imaginary circle going around the middle of the Earth, the same distance from the North and South Poles.

executive branch *n.*—the president and his staff. It is one of the three branches of federal government in the United States.

explore *v.*—to search out new places. *Example:* Christopher Columbus is the famous <u>explorer</u> who "discovered" America.

export *v.*—1) to sell something to someone outside your country. 2) *n.* something sold to another country.

fertile *adj.*—able to produce crops or offspring.

feudalism *n.*—the system of government during the Middle Ages where a lord granted protection to a group of people in return for part of their earnings (which in those days meant crops).

freedom *n.*—the ability to say and do what you want.

geography *n.*—the natural, physical features of a region.

goods *n.*—stuff that is bought and sold. In social science, it is used in the phrase "<u>goods</u> and services" to describe the products of an economy.

government *n.*—the political system by which a city, state, or country is ruled.

hemisphere *n.*—one of the two "halves" of the world divided by the equator. *Note:* The Northern <u>Hemisphere</u> contains the North Pole, and the Southern <u>Hemisphere</u> contains the South Pole.

hieroglyph *n.*—from ancient Egypt, a picture that represents words and ideas.

immigrate *v.*—to move to a foreign country.

import *v.*—1) to bring something from one country into another. 2) *n.* something brought from one country into another.

income *n.*—the money one earns at a job.

indentured *adj.*—contracted to. *Example:* Many people came to this country as <u>indentured</u> servants. To pay their way here, they signed contracts that said they would serve a master for a period of years, after which they would be free.

independence *n.*—freedom; not reliant on others.

industry *n.*—a group of related businesses. *Example*: When I grow up I want to work in the video game <u>industry</u>.

inhabitant *n.*—someone who lives in particular place. *Example:* I am an <u>inhabitant</u> of Boston, Massachusetts.

interact *v.*—to affect each other.

interdependent *adj.*—reliant on one another.

invent *v.*—to create.

judicial branch *n.*—the system of courts in the U.S. *Note*: The <u>judicial branch</u> is one of the three branches of government.

justice *n.*—1) the act of laws being carried out. 2) *n.* fairness.

labor *n.*—1) workforce. 2) *v.* to work.

latitude *n.*—the distance north or south of the equator, measured in degrees.

legend *n.*—the explanations of the symbols on a map.

liberty *n.*—freedom.

longitude *n.*—the distance east and west of the prime meridian, measured in degrees.

majority *n.*—the biggest group of people. *Note*: In the U.S., the <u>majority</u> rules, but the minority also has rights.

manufacture *v.*—to assemble; to make.

migration *n.*—the movement of a large group of people from one place to another.

militia *n.*—trained soldiers ready to fight at a moment's notice; an "on call" army.

minority *n.*—the smaller group of people.

monarchy *n.*—rule by a king or queen.

motto *n.*—a slogan or saying, usually used for self-identification. *Example*: The Texas state <u>motto</u> is "Don't mess with Texas."

nation *n.*—a country; people who live on the same land and have the same government.

native *adj.*—born in a particular place. *Example:* My dad is a <u>native</u> of Boston. He was born on the South Side in 1962.

navigate *v.*—to direct something (usually a ship) from one point to another.

oppress *v.*—to prevent people from doing what they want to do.

patriotism *n.*—love of one's country. *Note*: <u>Patriotism</u> is similar to nationalism, but nationalism has a negative connotation because it means one thinks less of other countries, as well.

persecute *v.*—to treat people very badly, usually because of their race or religion.

petition *n.*—a written document making a request. *Example:* I signed a <u>petition</u> that begged the owners of the Red Sox not to build a new stadium. We love Fenway!

population *n.*—the number of people who live in a given place.

prejudice *n.*—a negative attitude toward a group, race, or religion, held for no reason.

prime meridian *n.*—the reference line for measuring longitude that passes through Greenwich, England.

producer *n.*—in economics, the person or group of people who make the goods and provide the services. *Note*: In economics, producer is the "opposite" of *consumer*.

product *n.*—something that is made or manufactured.

profit *n.*—the money one makes from selling something. *Example*: It cost Bette $3.00 to make that cake. She sold it for $7.00. That's a $4.00 profit!

prohibit *v.*—to not allow, to forbid. *Example:* A sign at the public pool says cannonballs from the high dive are prohibited.

propaganda *n.*—information that is supposed to make someone believe something; often an exaggeration of fact or just "one side of the story."

protect *n.*—to defend against attack.

protest *v.*—1) to object strongly. 2) *n.* demonstration in the streets against something.

purchase *v.*—to buy.

reform *n.*—the improvement of laws or customs.

region *n.*—an area of land with blurry boundaries. *Example:* The Northeast region of the United States is marked by rocky soil and cold temperatures.

religious freedom *n.*—the ability to practice the religion of your choice, be it Christianity, Judaism, Islam, or any other faith.

Representatives, House of *proper noun*—one of two parts of the U.S. Congress. *Note*: In the House of Representatives, states are proportionally represented: the greater the state's population, the more representatives.

reservation *n.*—land set aside by the government for a specific purpose (in this country, usually for Native Americans).

respect *v.*—to hold in honor. The U.S. system of government is based on people respecting each other's differences.

responsibility *n.*—something required, an obligation.

revolution *n.*—the overthrow of one government by a new one.

right *n.*—as a citizen, something that is obligated to you. In the Declaration of Independence, rights of Americans include "life, liberty, and the pursuit of happiness."

risk *n.*—the possibility of suffering loss.

rural *adj.*—pertaining to the country (not the city).

scarce *adj.*—in short supply; not enough of something to go around to everyone who wants it.

Senate *proper noun*—one of two parts of the U.S. Congress. *Note*: Each state, regardless of its size, is represented by two senators in the Senate.

services *n.*—labor. In social studies, it is used in the phrase "goods and services" to describe the products of an economy.

risk *n.*—the possibility of suffering loss.

rural *adj.*—pertaining to the country (not the city).

scarce *adj.*—in short supply; not enough of something to go around to everyone who wants it.

Senate *proper noun*—one of two parts of the U.S. Congress. *Note*: Each state, regardless of its size, is represented by two senators in the Senate.

services *n.*—labor. In social science, it is used in the phrase "goods and services" to describe the products of an economy.

settlement *n.*—a small community in a new land.

settler *n.*—a person who establishes residence a new land.

shelter *n.*—a structure that offers protection from the weather.

slave *n.*—a person who is owned by another person.

state *n.*—a group of people under one government; usually a state is part of a country.

stereotype *n.*—an unfair generalization of a group of people.

suburban *adj.*—pertaining to an area close to the city, almost always a residential area.

supply and demand *n.*—a law of economics used in a market economy. *Note:* When demand for a product goes up, its supply must also increase, or the product will get more expensive.

surrender *v.*—to give up.

tax *n.*—money paid by citizens that goes to fund their government.

technology *n.*—things learned through science that we apply to the real world.

timeline *n.*—a special graph that shows events along a line, in the order they occurred.

tolerant *adj.*—allowing people to live by codes and customs that are different from the norm.

trade *n.*—1) the buying and selling of goods and services. 2) *v.* to give something and get something in return.

tradition *n.*—a way of doing things, passed down from generation to generation. (See the definition for *customs*.)

transportation *n.*—anything that moves something from here to there. *Example*: Planes, trains, and cars are forms of transportation.

treason *n.*—the crime of being a traitor; the betrayal of a government.

truce *n.*—a temporary fighting stoppage. *Note*: Wars usually have a bunch of truces before somebody finally surrenders for good.

tyranny *n.*—a government in which one person rules over everyone, and that one person is not very nice.

unalienable right *n.*—a right that can never be taken back or ignored.

union *n.*—a group of individuals who band together to protect their interests.

urban *adj.*—an inner-city area.

volunteer *n.*—1) someone who does something for a good cause, usually without pay. 2) *v.* to join a cause of your own volition.

Word Whiz List

Science

amphibian *n.*—a cold-blooded animal that breathes with gills when it's young, and with lungs when it's older.

annual *adj.*—yearly.

astronomy *n.*—the study of the universe.

atmosphere *n.*—the air surrounding the Earth.

attract *v.*—to draw closer. *Example*: Magnets <u>attract</u> some metals. *Note*: The opposite of <u>attract</u> is *repel*.

biodegradeable *adj.*—able to be broken down by natural processes.

camouflage *n.*—disguise. *Example*: Some animals use <u>camouflage</u> to hide from predators.

canyon *n.*—a chasm with steep cliffs on either side.

carbon dioxide *n.*—a gas made of one carbon and two oxygen atoms. It is what you breathe out during respiration.

cell *n.*—the building block of a living organism.

characteristic *n.*—feature; quality. *Example:* Pick the <u>characteristics</u> that best describe the cheetah.

circulation *n.*—in biology, the movement of blood around the body.

classify *v.*—to organize in groups. In science, animals and plants are <u>classified</u> into groups according to their physical characteristics.

condensation *n.*—moisture that collects as liquid or ice.

conduct *v.*—to help something, like electricity, go from one place to another.

conservation *n.*—the protection and preservation of natural resources.

constellation *n.*—a group of stars. *Example*: Orion and the Big Dipper are <u>constellations</u>.

decay *v.*—to break down; to decompose (see below).

decompose *v.*—to break down. In science, it usually refers to dead animals and plants <u>decomposing</u>.

density *n.*—the amount of something there is in a given unit of area or volume.

dissolve *v.*—to disintegrate into tiny particles and mix into a liquid. (See the definition for *soluble*.)

diversity *n.*—variety. *Example*: The Earth supports a <u>diversity</u> of living organisms.

eclipse *n.*—the blockage of light from the sun. *Example*: A solar

eclipse is caused by the moon passing between the Earth and the sun.

ecology *n.*—the science that studies how living things interact with their environment.

ecosystem *n.*—a group of plants, animals, and environmental factors that affect one another.

endangered *adj.*—threatened. *Note:* In science, endangered is usually used to describe animals threatened with becoming extinct.

energy *n.*—1) usable heat. 2) electricity.

environment *n.*—a person's, animal's, or plant's surroundings.

erosion *n.*—the process of wearing something away a little at a time.

evaporation *n.*—the process of liquid changing to gas.

evolve *v.*—to change from one thing into something different (usually, something better). The theory of evolution is based on the fact that animals evolve over time to better take advantage of their environment.

expand *v.*—to grow.

experiment *n.*—a test performed to prove something.

external *adj.*—on the outside.

extinct *n.*—died out. *Example:* Every year thousands of animals become extinct, never to be seen again.

food chain *n.*—a series of animals and plants that eat each other; the cycle of life.

fossil *n.*—the imprint or the remains of an animal from an earlier age, usually left in rock.

friction *v.*—rough rubbing. *Example:* The friction between tectonic plates causes earthquakes.

galaxy *n.*—a large group of stars. *Example:* The Earth is in the Milky Way galaxy.

gas *n.*—a form of matter with molecules that are farther apart than the molecules of a liquid or a solid. A gas has no shape and can expand to fill a container. It is typically invisible and sometimes has an odor.

gene *n.*—the part of a cell that determines the different characteristics of an organism.

generation *n.*—a group of organisms all about the same age; one stage in a series starting with one ancestor.

grassland *n.*—an area covered in grass, often used to graze cattle.

gravity *n.*—the force that draws objects to the Earth.

habitat *n.*—the place where an animal or plant lives.

hazard *n.*—danger. *Example:* Using a Bunsen burner without safety goggles can be a hazard to your health.

hibernation *n.*—a state of inactivity through the winter.

humidity *n.*—moisture in the air.

hypothesis *n.*—a theory to be either proved or disproved with an experiment. *Example:* Create an experiment to test the hypothesis that water evaporates when it gets very hot.

identical *adj.*—exactly alike; the same.

igneous rock *n.*—rock that is made of hardened liquified rock (magma). *Example:* Basalt is an igneous rock.

is involved with breathing?

investigate *v.*—to study; to look into.

life cycle *n.*—the process of progressing from birth to death.

liquid *n.*—a substance can be either a solid, a liquid, or a gas. Liquid flows, like water (which is, of course, a liquid), is denser than gas, but less dense than a solid.

lunar *adj.*—having to do with the moon.

magnetic *adj.*—having the ability to attract other things.

magnify *v.*—to make bigger. *Example:* Microscopes are used to magnify our view of tiny things.

mammal *n.*—a warm-blooded animal, usually with hair, that gives birth to live offspring.

mass *n.*—bulk; size. *Example:* What is the mass of the following objects?

matter *n.*—stuff; something that takes up space.

measure *v.*—to find the size or shape of something.

metamorphic rock *n.*—igneous or sedimentary rock that is changed into another kind of rock because of extreme pressure. *Example:* Marble is a metamorphic rock; it is smashed and heated limestone.

metamorphosis *n.*—a change from one thing to another. *Example:* A caterpillar must go through a metamorphosis to become a butterfly.

meteor *n.*—a piece of matter from outer space that enters the Earth's atmosphere, forming a streak of light behind it.

mineral *n.*—a natural substance, often mined for use by humans. *Example:* Coal and diamonds are both minerals.

natural resources *n.*—products of the Earth that people use to make their lives better.

observe *v.*—to watch closely.

orbit *n.*—the path of one heavenly body (like the moon) around another (like the Earth).

organism *n.*—a living thing. *Examples*: Plants, animals, and fungi are all organisms.

oxygen *n.*—an element that animals need to survive. *Example:* When humans breathe, we take in oxygen and breathe out carbon dioxide.

photosynthesis *n.*—the process plants use to turn sun, water, and carbon dioxide into food.

pollinate *v.*—to introduce pollen to a plant, which allows it to produce offspring.

pollute *v.*—to introduce harmful stuff into an environment.

population *n.*—the number of one kind of organism in a given habitat.

precaution *n.*—safety measure.

precipitation *n.*—rain, snow, sleet, or hail.

predator *n.*—an animal that hunts other animals for food.

predict *v.*—to guess at an outcome. *Example:* I predict that the Boston Red Sox will win the World Series sometime in the next five years.

prevent *v.*—to stop.

prey *n.*—the animal or animals a predator hunts for food.

properties *n.*—attributes.

recycle *v.*—to use again.

properties *n.*—attributes.

recycle *v.*—to use again.

reduce *v.*—to make smaller.

reflect *v.*—to send back an image, sound, or light. *Example:* The lights in the living room <u>reflected</u> off the computer screen, making it hard to see the video game I was playing.

renewable *adj.*—able to be used again or replaced by new growth. *Example*: Trees are <u>renewable</u> resources because new ones can always be grown.

reproduction *n.*—the act of producing offspring.

reptile *n.*—a cold-blooded animal that breathes with lungs and is usually covered with scales.

respiration *n.*—the act of breathing; inhaling and exhaling.

revolve *v.*—to move around on an axis; to orbit.

season *n.*—one of the four natural periods of the year: spring, summer, winter, and fall.

sedimentary rock *n.*—rock formed from compressed sediments. *Example*: Sandstone and limestone are <u>sedimentary rocks</u>. Sandstone is made from sand; limestone is made from fragments of sea creatures.

solar system *n.*—the sun, the group of planets, and the other heavenly bodies surrounding our sun. *Note: solar means sun.*

solid *n.*—a firm substance. *Note:* A substance can be either a <u>solid</u>, a liquid or a gas. A <u>solid</u> has a definite shape and weight. It has the highest density of the three forms of matter.

species *n.*—a group of organisms that can mate and have offspring.

structure *v.*—1) to arrange in an organized way. *Example:* <u>Structure</u> your answer according to the directions given. 2) *n.* something arranged in a definite pattern or system.

survive *v.*—to live on despite tough circumstances. The theory of evolution is based on "<u>survival</u> of the fittest." That means the organisms best equipped to live in a particular habitat will <u>survive</u> and have offspring.

system *n.*—an organization of parts that works together as a whole. *Example:* Our solar <u>system</u> is made up of nine planets orbiting the sun.

telescope *n.*—a device used to see things too far away to see with the naked eye (like other planets and galaxies).

temperature *n.*—the measure of how hot or cold something is.

texture *n.*—the feel of a surface. *Example*: Paper has a smooth <u>texture</u>. Sandpaper has a rough <u>texture</u>.

theory *n.*—a proposed reason why something is what it is. *Example*: Kevin's <u>theory</u> that the sun was a big, glowing breath mint was interesting, but wrong.

trait *n.*—a characteristic that makes something unique.

vapor *n.*—gas formed from something that is usually a liquid.

velocity *n.*—how fast something goes.

vibrate *v.*—to jiggle back and forth really fast.

waste *n.*—the stuff that is left over.

wetland *n.*—a marsh or swampy area saturated with water.

Also Available

20-Minute Learning Connection:
Massachusetts Elementary School Edition

Crusade in the Classroom:
How George W. Bush's Education Reforms
Will Affect Your Children, Our Schools

**Parent's Guide to Massachusetts State
4th Grade Tests,** Second Edition